Discover the Wonder
In your Life.

Move through the Darkness
Into the Light.

Learn from the Butterfly.

Shelagh Kennett

An Evolving Love Story

15 Insights on the Road to Own Who You Are Becoming

SHELAGH KENNETT

◆ FriesenPress

One Printers Way
Altona, MB R0G 0B0
Canada

www.friesenpress.com

Illustrator: https://www.suecoleman.ca
Written permission to use this beautiful art work given by Sue Coleman.

ACKNOWLEDGEMENTS: I started collecting inspiring quotes decades ago; I loved how
they captured snippets of wisdom in so many delightful ways. I noted them in margins
of books, journals and on scraps of paper. To all the amazing authors I have shared in my
book – thank you for feeding my soul, especially during my most difficult times. Please
know that great care, research and cost has been incurred to ensure accuracy. For any that
have been imperfectly worded or attributed, my sincerest apologies. Shelagh Kennett

ISBN
978-1-03-832606-5 (Hardcover)
978-1-03-832605-8 (Paperback)
978-1-03-832607-2 (eBook)

1. SELF-HELP, MOTIVATIONAL & INSPIRATIONAL

Distributed to the trade by The Ingram Book Company

To my four amazing children who inspired me to keep on believing,
And without whom this book would not have been possible,
There are no words to express my gratitude and love.

To all my family and friends who
"moved through the darkness into the light" with me.

And

To everyone who is prepared to love themselves enough
to enable you to believe in new dreams.

Thank you with all my heart

Table of Contents

INTRODUCTION

Do not now seek the answers . . . Live the questions now.
Perhaps you will then gradually, without noticing it, live along
some distant day into the answer.

—Rainer Maria Rilke (1875-1926), *Letters to a Young Poet*,
translated by M.D. Herter Norton
Austrian Poet & Novelist

ALL OF OUR LIVES ARE different and yet the template is surprisingly similar. The opportunity to rise above the intersection of hopeless and meaningful is available to all of us. It is the work of our soul on the road to authenticity and is a path worth discovering. This path is where we find the meaning that will light the way ahead; the tools are gratitude, hope, humility, courage, and trust. Through it all, they release the ultimate answer: self-love.

When it feels as if a jet plane has just crashed over the roof of your house and you don't know where to begin to pick up the pieces, or a life altering event has crushed your entire self-image and nothing in life makes sense, how can you find your way?

One of the major moments in my life occurred when I heard the statistic that only one in four survived the cancer diagnosis I had just received; I decided that I had to be that lucky one. My four children ranged from one to seven, and up until then, I had assumed we would all share a long life of wonderful memories together. There was no way I could wrap my mind and heart around anything that might prevent this dream from happening. This was one of several bombshells in my life that I never saw coming.

Stories, with their power to enlighten and inspire, bring answers, but often only years later, after the pain of the moment has gone. In the end, all the answers lie within ourselves. Now, so many years later, and after a rewarding time as a career coach, I have shared stories about both my own life experiences and those of my clients. As I followed the thread of my life and that of others, I realized that we often miss our moments of heroism because these are also often moments clouded with emotion and despair. Looking back, I felt the courage in each story. Once we can fully appreciate our stories, we can own who we are becoming.

In addition, we need to have a deep respect for how many things we may never fully understand—as the beautiful quote above by Rainer Maria Rilke states, we need to live the questions. We can love ourselves through it all and discover building blocks in every chapter, as I have done in this book.

The design of the four week course I created as a career program manager became the model for this book. It is divided into three sections: transformation, empowerment and renewal. Stories from my personal journey, and some stories from others, set the stage for the lessons. There are five insights in each of these three sections.

It has taken years and extensive journaling for me to uncover these insights, which now serve as a guide to a meaningful life. At the end of each chapter, I invite the reader to recall the stories in my book, draw parallels to their life, apply the concepts developed within the stories, and consider a new call to action. The readers may even discover other unique insights as they remember their own personal stories. This will further enhance one's ability to own who they are becoming.

I witnessed this process when I was a career program manager and counselor to hundreds of people from all over the world. It was during this time that I discovered there is an incredible strength within each of us. If we can make the shift from being blindsided by life and blaming ourselves to believing in a new dream and forgiving ourselves, we can embrace just exactly how unique we are and always have been.

Although all my clients came to improve their job-finding skills, almost all of their feedback referenced a valuable transformation, empowerment, and renewal of self-love. Often the real blocks to their success and happiness were caused by the stories they told themselves that limited their beliefs about what was possible and the endings they had already written.

Below are two comments from clients who attended my training over the years.

"I have never until now used the word "empowering" in association with anything to do with myself. Yet that is the only word to (succinctly) describe my time in your program." (Lawyer, recovering alcoholic, living and working at the Salvation Army to help others)

"I have never forgotten your kindness, warmth and genuine optimism, nor its continuing influence on my spirit, even after no longer being there in the program. Thank you for your real tools and encouragement to alter perceptions. Thank you for the support that helped me from disappearing into despair more than I already had." (Art Therapist)

This book is an evolving love story to myself. It is for anyone with a lost dream and for all who dream of a brighter tomorrow. So many are lost and lacking purpose in an epidemic of loneliness, anxiety and broken dreams. May these stories lead you, the reader, to enlightened moments in your life that enable you to discover a new dream.

Part 1

Transformation Is
Never Optional

Transformation happens every day in little and big ways.
You are in charge of the pace. We are always in a state of
transformation. How we respond to the events in our lives
is a choice. How we interpret our stories is very personal.
Throughout the journey we need to become our own best
friend. Stories, mine and yours, are memorable. They imprint
messages in our minds and on our hearts. Slowly, we become
the observer, lessons emerge, and we transform. As you read
the chapters of my transformational journey, allow them
to intertwine with your stories; draw parallels to your own
life and decide on your own call to action. Perhaps you will
slowly grow to transform your life and continue to make new
choices on the road to owning who you are becoming.

Chapter 1

The Die Is Cast

You're braver than you believe,
stronger than you seem and
smarter than you think.

—Carter Crocker and Karl Geurs, *Pooh's Grand Adventure:*
The Search for Christopher Robin
1997 American Animated Musical Adventure Comedy Drama Film

THIS WONDERFUL QUOTE HAS ALWAYS warmed my heart on so many levels. It is such a simple, powerful statement that I believe we all struggle with our whole life. If only we could see ourselves as we truly are, magnificent heroic human beings doing our best with what we have on any given day. It has inspired me to take the time to consider all of who I am, how I got this way, and the ways I have been blessed with so many gifts that helped to carry me through difficult new beginnings in my life.

A quote I always remember when I think about who I am is from Steve Jobs, who once said, "you can only connect [the dots] looking backward."[1] This might lead some to think we will only arrive at our peak of wisdom and self-knowledge many years later. However, if we take the time to

---

1 Steve Jobs, Stanford University commencement address (speech, Standford University commencement ceremony, Standford, CA, June 12, 2005), retrieved from "'You've got to find what you love,' Jobs says," *Standford Report*, June 12, 2005, https://news.stanford.edu/stories/2005/06/youve-got-find-love-jobs-says.

explore the many stages in our lives, we can start to connect those dots sooner. We can come to realize that our life is an incredible journey of "connected dots," each one contributing to the whole. In this way, there will be passages of wisdom whereby we can benefit from each mini-success and anticipate the next one. We can also reflect on how we grew in challenging times and developed our unique strengths. This creates trust in all of life and helps us see how owning who we are becoming is the way to our power, in the good times and the bad.

One story of me "connecting the dots" came in an experience with a wonderful book one of my daughters gave me twenty-five years ago, *Simple Abundance: A Daybook of Comfort and Joy* by Sarah Ban Breathnach. Sometimes I highlighted things or underlined sentences, and I even created references to favorite passages and wrote them down at the beginning of the book. I still read it every day and I am amazed that to this day, all these years later, I continue to "feel" things in new ways that didn't resonate with me until now. I find I often highlight new sentences as I engage with the book now. I had a different lens then. We are always becoming, and we will always be building on who we were and who we are now: braver, stronger, and smarter than before.

I encourage you to spend some quiet moments with yourself and let some of your early childhood memories flow into your conscious thoughts. They can remind you of who you really are, who you were before life became so overwhelming, and who you might be able to become again. I dedicate this chapter to all the people in my life who have contributed to who I am and all those who continue to make it possible for me to become anew each day.

The following reflections relate to my life and career, my family, and some inspiring ideas from favorite thinkers. I hope to show you that if we pause to connect with our early years when the "die was cast," it may guide us through some of the steps to transformation. As I look back over my early years, and even now, I understand so many ways that the "die was cast" to create who I am today. This empowers me with gratitude and humility and helps me to own who I am becoming.

Many years ago, an impressionable fourteen-year-old girl sat in a group with her peers listening to the leader, someone she had idolized from the time she was very young, a youth leader. This youth leader was a beautiful soft-spoken woman in her early twenties and newly married; her name was Joanie. The young girl's parents had previously hired Joanie to come on summer vacations to help with the children when she was much younger, so Joanie felt like family. The young girl wanted to be exactly like Joanie when she grew up. As she sat listening to her "lesson for the day" from the youth leader, Joanie shared how she had wanted a new dress for the holidays and how sorry she was feeling for herself that her family really couldn't afford it. Joanie recounted how she sat on the edge of her bed and opened her bible to a random page, believing it would take her to whatever message was intended for her that day. She then read what that scripture said: "Consider the lilies of the field, how they grow; they neither toil nor spin; and yet I say to you that even Solomon in all his glory was not arrayed like one of these. Now if God so clothes the grass of the field, which today is, and tomorrow is thrown into the oven, will He not much more clothe you, O you of little faith?"[2]

Wow! What a fateful moment, for such a perfect verse to come to her! What resonated about that story deep within this fourteen year old, and stayed with her forever, was how a quiet faith can help us navigate through each day if we are open to looking for answers. It laid the foundation for her that we are responsible to look for our own solutions, and we can trust that we will find them. Yes, this young girl was me.

Another story from my childhood that my mother used to tell, which of course goes back too far for me to personally remember, was the day she had to have that "you are old enough to know the truth" conversation about Santa Claus. I had come home from school and told her that all my friends said there is no Santa Claus. Apparently, after what my mom thought was a beautiful account of the meaning of Christmas and the origin of Santa Claus, I said, "Well, that is fine, but I am going to believe in Santa Claus anyway." This perhaps was a key indicator that at the age of about nine, the die was cast and I was destined to seek the magic in the mysteries of life, a trait that ultimately carried me through life's challenges. I was a believer

---

2 Mathew 6:28-30 (The New King James Version)

before I could see it, and this can make life easier sometimes. It doesn't always guarantee a happy ending, but it can help one navigate the rough spots by leaning on hope until the road becomes better. Optimism sustains one's energy longer than the alternative.

I also had a special connection with my dad. Many things I learned from him contributed to the ways the "die was cast" very early in my childhood, especially those lessons about learning from our challenges and embracing new beginnings. When I was thirteen my dad, who had been subject to depression, began his successful thirty-two-year-old journey of sobriety in Alcoholics Anonymous. He helped himself, and hundreds of others, stay sober until he took his last breath on this Earth. They called him the "grand old man."

Since my dad was allergic to alcohol and had given up drinking, he was called a "dry drunk." Therefore, I have no memory of ever seeing him drunk. However, he had not yet dealt with the other issues of him being an alcoholic. I vividly remember the heartbreaking challenges that came from watching my dad endure bouts of depression. It was difficult to share so much fun and joy and then, seemingly out of the blue, to see the "mask of depression" cover his face and leave him totally unable to engage in any kind of father/daughter interaction. Fortunately, his amazing psychiatrist followed his instinct and guided my dad to Alcoholics Anonymous.

By celebrating milestone birthdays at AA meetings and listening to people's stories of rebuilding their lives following a path of destruction, I learned a lot about what is possible when one commits to transforming themselves, no matter how deep they have sunk into despair. I was grateful our family had been able to escape a lot of those things. As my dad came to understand how best to manage his emotions and periods of depression, we all learned along with him. I also shared a delightful sense of humor with my dad; in addition, my love of quotes, beautiful poems, and continuous journaling was inspired by my dad's love of all these things.

My dad definitely came to own who he was becoming throughout his thirty-two years in the "fellowship" of Alcoholics Anonymous. He was more than a true inspiration. All these diverse qualities that my dad instilled in me are an integral piece of how the "die was cast" in me. They gave me many tools to successfully transform myself.

Several years later, I was excited to go on my first adventure from home to a satellite arm of McGill University, Macdonald College Campus—another foundational die-casting moment. It was out in the country away from Montreal where I had grown up. The first time I entered the connecting tunnel from the women's residences to the building of lecture halls I was on crutches. Extenuating circumstances had enabled me to begin my school years early and I was starting university at a young age; I had just spent a "sweet sixteen" summer following knee surgery in a full leg cast and was now so totally ready for this new experience. They had removed my kneecap, something typically reserved for professional football players and the like, but since I wasn't planning a career in sports, I was not concerned.

Looking back, there is no memory of hardship or thought of "why me?" What may have guided my optimistic perception of any accident or health issue can perhaps be attributed to my mother. Throughout my primary and secondary school years, I had already faced one knee surgery, two concussions, two animal attacks, a broken jaw and cheekbone, two severe lung infections, debilitating migraine headaches, and a split-open head requiring stitches. The family doctor had officially declared me "accident-prone."

Then, when I was faced with the prospect of a second knee operation requiring me to be in a cast most of the summer before university, my mother searched for a reassuring response. She said, "The universe must have something very special in mind for you. You are being tested and molded for something great." Some might think this was a rash take on facing so many challenges. Why not let a five-, ten-, or fifteen-year-old enjoy a little "poor me" time and take in some of the special privileges and benefits of being the "poor little sick girl?"

At a profoundly impressionable age, my mother had thus blessed me with what has become a lifelong approach to every area of my life. The die was cast for me to bring a level of positivity to everything that would happen to me in the future and to believe it had a purpose in my life. In fact, it was up to me to identify the role these events played in my life. I came to believe that adversity was always grooming me for something special. I learned that it was in the rough spots of one's life—when the rubber meets the road—that we discover who we really are, what we are really made of, and what we are really capable of overcoming and achieving.

Now fast-forward to the summer prior to my third year at McGill University when I marched around the house to band music. I had set my sights on being a majorette in my transition from the two years at the satellite college to my first year to McGill University. My mom, my "cheerleader extraordinaire," was an influence on my mindset my whole life, and she continues to be in her absence on this earth. In my quest to become a university majorette, she outdid herself again.

Some parents might have been unable to resist the need to be the "reality check." They might have been compelled to point out that just two years after having my kneecap removed and never having been a majorette, this might be a somewhat far-fetched goal. However, I don't remember my mom ever using words to hold me back on anything I aspired to do; becoming a majorette was just one example.

When I wasn't marching around the house to build up my knee muscles, I was learning how to twirl a baton in our backyard. To be a majorette would involve marching up and down a major hill in the middle of downtown Montreal. And yet, never once did my mom attempt to take away my dream, refer to what a long shot my being chosen was, or even suggest I may not be physically or technically capable of succeeding even if I was chosen. My vision of leading the band and marching through the streets of Montreal drove me to work hard all summer.

And so of course, as I write and remember this, my being a McGill University majorette was clearly one of my fondest dreams come true and one of my greatest memories of my university years. This support highlights the powerful effect a single person in our lives can have on our success and self-image. Once the die has thus been cast, this positive influence can last throughout our lives, and we may not even realize it until later—and perhaps only if we focus on "connecting the dots."

Sadly, the opposite can be true, and this is when we need to seek out all the missing links to positivity that did not form in our childhood. Learning at any age is influenced by the lens through which we view ourselves and our place in the world. Freud believed that the major development of one's personality is already formed by six years of age and that this can create a permanent imprint on a person's belief system.[3] My hope in writing this book is that the reader can come to realize that our belief system is not static and can be recreated and changed, similar to the ways our brain can. Just as we can find foundations of strength and self in the past, as the stories in our lives keep changing, with each new beginning, we can become stronger in ways we could not have imagined. This, in turn, can strengthen our ability to believe in possibilities. We can move beyond the influences of our early years and cast the die for our future selves as we continue to make deposits in our reservoir of positivity because, of course, we are braver, stronger, and smarter than we first thought!

I also took away an important lesson a few years ago when I took a writing course on "leaving a legacy" at Simon Fraser University. Coincidently, or perhaps not, the instructor was a former business associate, journalist, and writer whom I had not seen for over twenty years. The goal was to create a story and then add pictures, music, and poetry and ultimately deliver a presentation to the class. Most of the class was writing about the legacy of someone else, and I chose to honor my sister and write about what I titled "A Courageous Journey from Bankruptcy to a New Home at Seventy-Four." Two incredible gifts evolved from this decision to explore her new beginnings.

First, the jewel of completing this program: while searching for material from our past as sisters, I found a book I had treasured when I was ten. It was extraordinary that it had somehow managed to remain on my bookshelf after so many moves back and forth across the country. It was called *Odz 'n Enz*. This was a wonderful collection of inspirational poems compiled by Robert Parsons and quite beyond the understanding of a ten-year-old. However, there on the inside front cover was the printing of a ten-year-old with my name, phone number, and address, and I have no idea how it came to be mine.

On a much deeper level, I found myself thinking that no matter all the changes and influences that have impacted my life, I have always been

---

3 Pooja Dubey, "The First Six Years Form Your Personality But There Is Hope!" LinkedIn, January 17, 2020, https://www.linkedin.com/pulse/first-six-years-form-your-personality-hope-writer-pooja-dubey .

who I am, someone who cherishes beautiful, inspiring written messages. It is truly in my DNA. If we take the time to explore what makes us feel alive, we can make sure we seek it out often. Essentially, we will own it and become it.

However, the greater gift in writing about a seventy-four-year-old needing to find a new home came when I had wanted to identify with the challenges of my older sister downsizing. Now, after six years without her husband, who was her childhood sweetheart, she would be leaving the last home they lived in together before he died. She lived three thousand miles across the country from me in Toronto and sadly, I could not go there to help at the time. So instead I began to get rid of a multitude of my things too, just as she had to do, to be with her in spirit.

I had read that to have more in our lives, we need to create space for it, physically and metaphorically speaking. This process of sorting and downsizing also led me to uncover many journals, inspirational treasures, career-related memories, and sentimental keepsakes from my children, all of which I had long since forgotten I even had. Ultimately, these became what jump started the journey that brought me to write this book. Once again the die was cast; I discovered so many gifts that had set the foundation for me, and I was now on the road to a new adventure.

All these people and events in the stories I have shared in this chapter have shaped my thinking and they gave me the template of optimism for thriving in a life of challenges and new beginnings. I came to navigate many of them deep in my heart as "gifts"; I called them "character builders" of the most personal kind.

I hope these stories have inspired you to discover many character builders cast in your past and to think about how you can cast the die for your future self, too. However, all this doesn't mean it is easy holding on to an optimistic template. I share with you all one of the greatest tests to my philosophy in chapter two.

Insights to Own Who You Are Becoming – Building on Self-Knowledge

I encourage you to spend some quiet moments with yourself and let some of your early childhood memories flow into your conscious thoughts. They can remind you of who you really are, who you were before life became so overwhelming, and who you might be able to become again. Do you have a Santa Claus story? Was there a youth leader that created a habit for life in you? Can you remember the first time you set a big goal and how you made it happen?

The most empowering thing one can do is to take responsibility for one's own life; the most liberating thing one can do is decide that you have within you the power to become someone new every moment of every day. Remember you are braver, stronger, and smarter than you believe! Did your mother, father, or another special person inspire you to believe in your own abilities? Can you find that childlike courage again? In the end, it is only when we act on all the positivity we have learned from others and combine it with our own strength that the magic can happen.

Our belief system is not static. It is influenced by the stories in our lives, and as such we keep changing with each new beginning. Initially, we may not have been able to imagine how an experience could lead to such amazing outcomes. Can you write down one shift in your beliefs about people and life that recently enabled you to try something new?

Deep self-knowledge reveals the essence of our inner being and discovering it can feel like we are reconnecting with an old friend. Finding a treasured book I had when I was ten years old was a moment of uncovering deep self-knowledge. Can you think of one for you or how you might find it?

As you move through this book from transformation and empowerment to renewal, think about how you can build on the best of what you have learned throughout your life and how you can even benefit from the low points and challenging people as well. Start to write down your "build from the best" list whenever they come into your mind and heart. Create another list to reflect on how you also learned from negative experiences to set the stage for learning from all of life's lessons.

Notes to Own Who You Are Becoming:

Chapter 2

Life Is Fragile

We do not always have the freedom to choose the roles
we must play in this life, but we can choose how we are
going to play the roles we have been given.

—Jerry Sittser, *A Grace Disguised: How the Soul Grows through Loss*
American Professor Emeritus of Theology & Author

AS I LOOK BACK, I often think about how we tend to proceed as if we know what our day will hold and act accordingly. We rarely cherish moments with joy and gratitude in case they never come again; we assume they will. We believe that we are in control of so many things, but in fact, we are in control of very little.

This story begins on an ordinary day in my life as a busy mother with four small children aged one through seven. Their father left for work early, as he always did, and the little ones were happily playing with all their new toys. It was just two days after Christmas. This was the day that I had arranged for a babysitter to come for a few hours in the afternoon so that I could return some of the duplicate gifts and/or exchange some for better choices or sizes. This was a luxury I sometimes gave myself since trying to do these shopping chores with four busy little people seriously hampered my progress. In addition, after hosting the four grandparents and aunts and uncles for Christmas dinner and completing all the pre-Christmas activities of decorating, shopping, baking, wrapping and entertaining, a respite from motherhood was going to be a welcome break, even as I navigated the busy shopping malls. There was nothing about the day to lead me to believe that before it was over, my life as I knew it would change forever.

That evening, I had just returned from the hectic "two days after Xmas frenzy" in the stores and I had sent the babysitter home. All my children were very excited to see me and immediately dive into all the parcels; for them, it was like another Christmas event. Then, to top off their excitement, my mom arrived for a surprise visit after her workday to share a cup of tea and lend a hand, as the busy dinner hour would soon begin.

Our delightful time together was interrupted by a phone call from my babysitter who had forgotten to give me a message. As she spoke, I felt my heart racing and could not imagine how I would keep my composure when I hung up the phone. She had forgotten to tell me my doctor's office had called while I was out and they needed to see me right away. Only I knew what this likely meant. I thanked her for letting me know, slowly hung up, and wondered how I would quietly ask my mom to stay with the children while I went to the doctor's office before they closed for the day. Sensing it just might be great for me to have some extra moral support, she urged me to call back the sitter, who luckily could return to stay with my little ones. This would be the first of many times in the months ahead that I would be grateful that they were too young to understand the gravity of everything happening.

My mind was rapidly processing all the details in the past ten days and trying desperately not to get ahead of myself until I was with the doctor. Something that made this very difficult was that the doctor who had called was not my family doctor; he was filling in for him, as my family doctor was away on a family Christmas ski holiday. In fact, I had never gone to this doctor before and yet it was his nurse asking me to come in right away. What was making this so urgent? Every instinct within my being told me what I didn't want to believe must be true. It was just a five-minute drive to the doctor's office, but that was plenty of time to replay the entire conversation from my previous visit with my own doctor.

Just before Christmas, I noticed an insignificant "thing" on my upper right arm. When I showed it to my husband, I was surprised that he thought I should go see the doctor right away. It was such a busy time, being only one week before Christmas, and he usually downplayed these things. It was this "out of the norm" response that pushed me to get it checked out quickly. There are many times in our lives that we can look back and ask ourselves about the reason for a specific action—or the opposite, ask ourselves why we ignored something.

This became a "game changer" in my thinking. Only we can be responsible for our decisions. We have this tiny unexplainable thing called instinct, and it is important to slow down enough to allow it to guide us. We must never be too busy to take care of the "now," or we might find that there are no second chances to get it right.

When I arrived at my appointment with my cavalier family doctor to ask about my arm, he said, "This is nothing, but we have this philosophy in medicine: 'When in doubt, cut it out,' and I am not busy today." Of course he wasn't busy—it was just a week before Christmas and everyone was busy shopping, wrapping, baking, and attending school concerts.

While waiting for the freezing on my arm to kick in the doctor had shared what it *could* be but, in his opinion, certainly was not, a malignant melanoma. I had never heard this term, and my life had also been sheltered from having anyone close to me who had confronted cancer. Of all the things he told me, one phrase resonated: "There is virtually no known treatment and only one in four survive."

Ethically, sharing all this information with the patient was a dreadful faux pas; however, he was sure the small wart-like growth on my arm was nothing to cause anyone concern. It had not done any of the things typical of a melanoma; it had not grown in size or changed color, there had been no bleeding, and it was not causing any discomfort. However, it was new. I tried to hold the doctor's confidence that it was totally fine in my heart all through Christmas.

Now, with this new call from the doctor's office after Christmas, that confidence was gone. When my mom and I arrived, there were very few people in the waiting room since most people were preparing for New Year's Eve and recovering from Christmas. I was called in to see the doctor almost immediately, and of course, he didn't know what my doctor had already told me. I sensed how anxious he was when I entered his office. He stood up and said, "Let's take a look at your arm," perhaps to break the ice since he had never even met me and/or to stall the inevitable of telling me the results of the biopsy.

Once the doctor stated that it was a melanoma, I shared that I was aware that only one in four patients with this cancer survived. Of course he was shocked that I already knew these details. He then went straight to the next steps of how quickly they would schedule surgery and tried to undo the damage of the premature transparency from my family doctor. He said, "No one can know for sure how another person will progress with any illness." He did his best to instill a glimmer of hope in the situation.

I walked out past my mom in the waiting room and she knew without me telling her: the bottom line was I had cancer. I was reeling from the reality that I was no longer in control of my destiny, and I realized the plain and simple fact is none of us are. I was focused on the pending moment of how I would tell my husband, who might already be home now for dinner, and the conversations my poor Mom would face, as she would have to tell my dad and all the rest of the family.

There is simply no way to prepare for this kind of life-changing information. One minute I am looking after my children, and the next minute I am getting scheduled for surgery ten days later. Furthermore, there would be no way to know if I would be one of the one in four to survive until at least two weeks after the surgery.

The first appointment, on New Year's Eve, was with the plastic surgeon scheduled to do the surgery on January 6th. I remember thinking then that there are certain things we must all do alone, no matter how big our circle of family and friends might be. This was one of them. As I waited for the plastic surgeon to come into the examination room, I had told myself if he shared one positive thing, that is where I would focus my thoughts. He had a big task of undoing the frightening words my family doctor had stated.

The surgeon was very open, and he told me a lot of scary things that could happen or might already have happened in terms of how a melanoma can spread and how fast. But in all the bad news I heard him say, "We have climbed the first mountain; it's not in the lymph nodes yet, and that is good news." In that moment I adopted a personal mantra, "Where there is life, there is hope," and that piece of hope from the surgeon carried me through some of the very difficult days that were ahead. I was alive, I had hope, and today was all anyone had for sure, not just me. As I looked at my four children playing in the family room, I decided that I had to be the one in four that survived; I had to see them grow up.

My thoughts drifted back to the time when I was only sixteen facing a second knee surgery and my mom had said, "You must be destined for something special. The universe has chosen to build your character with these challenges." This seemed a bit of an extreme "character builder" that, given the choice, I would have chosen to leave out of my life! At thirty-one years of age, it was the first time that I had to confront my own mortality. The seeds of finding purpose in difficulties planted by my mom so many years ago were calling on me to rally and believe. How would I get past this new reality?

The surgery went well and I woke up to confirm to my delight that I could fully use my arm and there would be no reason I could not almost immediately lift my seventeen-month-old baby girl out of her crib and care for her. It was only seven o'clock in the morning and the hospital halls were quiet except for the nurses doing routine early morning checks on each room. I slowly walked down to the pay phones, giddy with the euphoric feeling one might feel after a big win in a sports event. This was before you could simply pull out your cell phone and text or call anyone from anywhere. I phoned my mom and dad to share with them how great I felt. My dad answered and as we talked he called out to my mom, "It's Shelagh, and I think she has been drinking." That was especially funny considering I had never had a first drink and my dad had been in AA for years! The perspective this moment gave me then, and all these years later, of what the joy of being alive really feels like, was incredible. Clearly in that brief phone call I was fully present in the "now," and I was so excited to be alive!

If we are lucky, when faced with significant illnesses, life gently eases us back to health, and sometimes it is best that we only know what the challenge for today will be. It is easier to climb the mountain one day at a time. Life is fragile, and we can never know at what moment we will be blindsided and called upon to dig deep inside for hope, courage, and trust in the unknown.

What we do know for sure is that transformation is never optional. We will emerge a different person at the end of each new challenge. There will be new respect for life, humility in understanding how little we can control or predict, and a need to develop a deep trust in the universe to find peace on our way to renewal.

This was the beginning of two years of fifty-four Bacille Calmette-Guérin (BCG) vaccinations delivered weekly, biweekly, and finally every month. I was actively involved with amazing doctors and nurses and met so many brave patients each time I went to the cancer clinic. Although I was experiencing challenging side effects that grew more intense throughout the two years, I was confident that ultimately I would be alright. I had the benefit of playing an active role in my journey back to health.

Looking back on this time in our lives, I know it was a great strain on my husband and the extended family. Often so much attention was focused on me and it was sometimes as if I was the "hero" in the drama. Rarely would someone ask how other family members were doing. I remember overhearing my husband say on the telephone when my mother-in-law had phoned to see how I was doing, "She is OK and she will always be OK, so you don't need to phone every day and ask anymore."

At one point my mother-in-law said, "Don't you think all these treatments are a bit overkill?" All this was totally understandable, and she just wanted to take the worry away from her son and the burden of all those trips to the cancer clinic away from me. My husband would just have preferred to never have had a wife who had cancer, and I wished he would share his feelings with a friend. Most of the time it was just that "elephant in the room" that we never talked about.

I went to the Cancer Clinic on Fridays. It was in the second year that the appointments changed to monthly. Family and friends would even forget I had gone, and gradually it wasn't even acknowledged anymore. During this time, the same cavalier family doctor from earlier said, "You need to think of this like an allergy shot now and get on with your life." However, for anyone who has gone into a cancer clinic, it is not something you can easily brush off at the end of the day after you have been a patient in the waiting room for several hours. You are surrounded by people who are all in so many stages of recovery and the loved ones who accompanied them always carry so much anguish on their faces. For this reason, I preferred to go alone and only deal with my own emotions. This clearly was in no way "like an allergy shot" to the active participant.

This all led to years of acting as if everything was just fine. We did not talk about my visits to the cancer clinic or the impact of seeing so much tragedy, knowing so many people I saw there would likely never get better. Sometimes I had deep concerns that I might not be alright and worried about how my family would manage. My children were too young to be aware of any of these realities, and my husband's coping mechanism was to just get on with our lives. Many years later, I reflected on a heartbreaking outburst. I would come to understand for the first time that even as the heart/brain connections override the feelings deep within your soul, you will never be able to predict the moment the soul will become visible and let you know the depth of its pain. I believe knowing your heart's truth like this is part of the process of owning who you are becoming.

This moment came a few years after I had completed my treatments. A young classmate of my oldest daughter, only eleven years old and with a twin sister, became ill with terminal cancer. He had already won the hearts of all his classmates with his wonderful love of life. I was deeply touched when I heard he had cancer and was overcome with gratitude and humility that I seemed to be past my cancer now. I could not imagine what it would be like if one of my four children had cancer. It made me realize how great a heartache it must have been for my brave parents following my initial surgery and all during my two years of treatment. At the time, I was too involved with my treatments to have this level of empathy for my family.

I didn't know this family well, but I became totally drawn into their heartache. I just thought of how it would have been for me if my daughter had cancer instead of me. It was Christmas time when we learned about this classmate's diagnosis, and I was experiencing a flood of memories remembering that dramatic Christmas season I found out about my cancer. It became quickly evident that I was not able to discuss how blessed our lives were and how hard it must be for this young boy's parents with my husband. He preferred to never go back to those memories as if they had never happened.

The boy passed away, and then came the memorial service. I wanted to be there, and I knew it would upset my husband to share that I was going to it, especially since his family did not even relate to the practice of funerals. I left the service and went to my parents' home, thinking I would just have a little meditative time to myself and fill myself with gratitude for my own health. They were away on a winter holiday.

However, something happened in the solitude of my parent's home. It was as if all the suppressed emotions, especially throughout the two years of treatments and trips to the cancer clinic, exploded in a single moment. I began to cry uncontrollably; it lasted for a long time. Sooner or later, your soul's deepest emotions will find a way to get your attention.

This was a positive turning point in my transformation. The emotions connected to life-changing events, like dealing with our mortality or someone else's, remind us that life can change at a moment's notice. They cannot and should not be suppressed forever. We might need to seek professional help, or align with support groups sharing similar life experiences, to heal in the best possible way. However, the human spirit is amazingly resilient. Celebrate your milestone moments when you have climbed personal mountains. Create an arsenal of these successes and draw on them to better manage the next journey from transformation through empowerment to renewal.

Remember that life is fragile, change is inevitable, and we will continue to be asked to rise to new occasions and to transform. Each time, we will emerge stronger. All these years later, I understood that this complete meltdown after the funeral was the outpouring of those real feelings I carried in my soul during my treatments. I realized that you cannot fault one for not appreciating your needs if you do not share them. Looking back, I also believed this was a cry for help that no one, not even me, understood at the time. Open communication with loved ones throughout a life-threatening illness is such an integral part of healing. The challenge is that not everyone shares the same coping styles; some internalize their fears, and others need to talk about them. How can we find that middle ground to continue living one day at a time, especially when we are unable to step into another's shoes?

It is a constant challenge for each of us to set aside time every day to listen to the quiet whispers from deep within our soul. No one else can do this for us. There may be reasons, good ones, important ones, that we need to knowingly suppress our feelings; it could be family, career, health, finances, or any number of factors. As you read about what happened to me when I significantly suppressed my emotions, take a moment to pause and reflect on your life. You can only truly own and value the milestone moments when you climb personal mountains if you know what they are.

Know that without intentional love, care, and time for your soul's deepest needs and desires, there will be a price, a loss. Recovery may come at a later date. Enlightenment and recharging your soul so you can reach your greatest potential can be postponed. However, the ability to live those years authentically will be lost forever.

Amidst the journey from helplessness to hopefulness, we do, in fact, always have power. How we respond to life is always a choice, and that choice can be the difference maker in creating a journey that is more manageable and meaningful.

This is real life, not a story where we write and control the endings. Maybe our imagination can't even perceive an ending with a new beginning. Validate your fears and low points in life. Recognize the value in remembering what you have overcome, as well as what you may have supressed and denied that your soul needs you to give a voice to now. Celebrate your courage, as it is not a small thing in the face of adversity.

No matter how much time goes by, I am always going to be a Cancer Survivor. This can be the worst thing that has ever happened to me, or it can be a gift. It is up to me to choose how I will label it. Life is fragile and my soul needs my attention.

Insights to Own Who You Are Becoming –
Recovering Is Not the Same as Curing

"Where there is life there is hope." This is the mantra I embraced at the peak of uncertainty following my cancer diagnosis; it has been a profound gift that has supported me through many new beginnings. Has there been a time in your life when either you or a loved one was confronted with their own mortality? Until we are walking in those shoes, "through the valley of the shadow of death,"[4] we cannot know the potential of our strength in adversity; it can surprise us in the best possible ways. The mantra that emerges from deep within can become the one that sustains you throughout the rest of your life. Do you have one? Can you create one now?

The precarious uncertainty of one's health is a fact of life. We rarely think about it until we must. When I told my neighbor I was doing great, she said, "But it is the uncertainty of it all." However, I believed that I was the lucky one; I knew each day that my health was a gift, but she lived with the misconception that we were different. Her life was uncertain too. There was no changing my diagnosis and no amount of worry was going to change the facts. However, I could take charge of my thoughts and make daily decisions to stay in the present moment and find joy; I could let go of the unknown that often overwhelms so many people. How do you stay in the present moment?

Think about some of the ways you have risen to life's challenges and what helped you to cope. Maybe you have forgotten your moments of greatness and how courageous you have already been in the past. Get in touch with your childlike trust; perhaps it grew within a miracle you overlooked.

The most important action each of us can take is to be intentional about our physical and mental health. Plan to have things that are new and/or not normal checked, be responsible about follow-up, and trust there will be solutions. Find "safe" listeners so we can voice our fears and validate that they are "normal." All of these activities can be difference makers as we strive to manage our mind, body, and soul health concerns.

---

4 Psalm 23: 4 (New KJV)

Chapter 3

Learn to Listen to Your Soul

For reason, ruling alone, is a force confining;
and passion, unattended, is a flame that burns to its own destruction.
Therefore let your soul exalt your reason to the height of passion,
that it may sing.

—Kahlil Gibran (1883-1931), "On Reason and Passion," *The Prophet*
Lebanese American Writer, Poet & Visual Artist

I BELIEVE THAT THERE IS something deep within each of us that patiently waits for opportunities to get our attention. I call this our soul. How well do you know your soul, and have you found the best ways to connect with it? In order to truly transform, we need to be open to going beyond our conscious day-to-day thoughts that are primarily controlled by reason. Passion can be suppressed, but it cannot be ignored. Also, we are not aware of over ninety per-cent of the thinking that drives our decisions and behaviors; this thinking lies in our subconscious mind. Inside you may be asking yourself, "How will I know I am on the right path?" Subconsciously, you may even have found a way to hide from your truth. What must your soul do to reach you? Let me share a beautiful memory of when circumstances made it possible for my soul to align with my heart.

My brother-in-law had just picked me up at the airport in Toronto; I was there on a business trip. He could not have been any more special to me than if he was a blood brother. We had shared years and years of laughter, pure joy, sadness, loss, and spiritual growth. From the time I was fifteen and he and my sister were eighteen, we were a one-of-a-kind threesome; I recall so many special memories of the two of them up front and me riding in the backseat of their Volkswagen. Throughout my teenage years, they always took me along, and later on, we continued to share so many life experiences together.

All three of us shared a love of country music and as we drove along on the 401 Highway across Toronto to their home he said, "There's a special song I want to play for you." The song began; it was "Angels Among Us"[5] sung by Alabama (perhaps you know the song).

I looked out the window on the passenger's side hoping that he wouldn't see the tears pouring down my face. It might well have been the first time I felt safe enough to allow the deep pain inside me to flow out with abandon.

Then I heard him say, "Well, that's the last time I share one of my favorite songs with you." We both laughed together through the tears, and I tried to find my voice and the words to share with someone for the first time that I didn't think I could stay in my marriage. I had kept it deep inside me for such a long time and was so afraid to hear myself say it out loud.

My sister and her husband had gone through so many huge challenges with significant heartaches and losses in their parenting, business, and family life. Why couldn't I be like them? They had a deep faith and would have shared their last meal or penny with a stranger. I always referred to my sister as "my very own Mother Teresa." Still, I had wondered what they would think when I told them.

My brother-in-law just quietly said, "You need to follow your heart." There was no judgment, no barrage of questions, no criticism of me or my husband, no unsolicited advice, no opinion of any kind.

Although reading this now one might think that it seemed like a very simplistic response, I have never forgotten it to this day. The special music, which had always been a constant comfort to my soul, combined with a "safe" listener, made it possible for me to accept the truth deep within my soul: my marriage would not be able to last.

---

5 Alabama, "Angels Among Us," by Don Goodman and Becky Hobbs, recorded 1993, RCA Nashville, track 11 on *Cheap Seats*, compact disc.

That moment in the car driving back to my sister's home and the song "Angels Among Us" carried me through some incredibly dark years. I came to expect there would be angels everywhere whenever I needed them, just like that day in the car with my brother-in-law. I started to look for those serendipitous moments when the universe would find ways to show me that everything would somehow be alright, in time. You will see that I have even devoted a chapter to "Serendipity and Synchronicity," as well as one to "Angels Disguised as Strangers." In this case, though, my angel wasn't a stranger, but family.

It would be several years after this emotional drive and multiple moments of my poor soul trying to get my attention before my life would start to move forward in a dramatic way. One beautiful summer day on my way home from work, as I crossed the bridge where I would normally turn right, I took the left lane and drove to the beach to walk along the ocean. This had never happened before and it was not my normal pattern, as I had not yet been home for supper. The truth is that particular day I felt a deep ache in my heart and could not bring myself to go home. For someone who had spent a lifetime creating a home intended to bring peace, love and joy to everyone who visited and/or lived there, this was an extraordinary red flag that life was falling apart. I knew as I processed the feelings that something was very wrong and I needed help.

Shortly after that experience came the bizarre moment when deep inside I felt compelled to get in my car and drive away. I recall walking with a close friend of my husband's; their families grew up together, so he was like a brother to her. She had also become a dear friend to me and gave phenomenal support to both of us as we navigated the painful journey leading up to our divorce. I said, "I need to go away."

She replied quietly, "Yes, maybe a few days in Victoria (a short ferry trip from my home) would be good."

"No," I said, "away, really away." To leave my children, even though they were now young adults in their twenties, was as uncharacteristic for me as snow in July. My entire self-image was tied to my family and my children.

How does a person, nicknamed Snow White by her children's friends, find herself embarking on a thirteen-hour drive alone away from the joys of her life? Was it a midlife crisis after her mother died? Could it be the white-collar court case her husband recently lost, along with his promising career and lucrative retirement package? Was it the exciting $200,000 proposal she was so close to securing that had been abandoned by her three male colleagues, also resulting in her losing her position in their company? What finally took this Cancer Survivor, Disney-loving, Hallmark enthusiast out of her well-known mindset of "where there is life, there is hope?"

I had given a letter I had written to my husband saying that we were not going to make it in our marriage and I needed to go away for awhile. Our community would have voted us the most likely in the neighborhood to reach our fiftieth wedding anniversary; therefore, this could be deemed to be shocking. What was even more beyond understanding was that me, a woman dedicated to her four children and giving them a happy home, could even think of leaving like this, as if she did not care about the pain she would cause her children, never mind her husband. However, behind that point of hopelessness, when one only feels failure and regret, where one's actions may seem sudden, can be years of silent sadness. This action that seemed to come out of nowhere happened gradually, the way water in rivers changes the shapes of rocks over time.

As I drove, I wasn't thinking about tomorrow or the next day; I was just in the moment and focused on a safe arrival to the home of my daughter now living in Alberta. A few days later, I left my car there and took a plane to join my sister in Toronto, now 3,000 miles from my other three children back home.

Together, like a pair of runaway teenagers, my sister and I flew to Prince Edward Island, where we had spent all our childhood summer holidays when we were growing up in Montreal, Quebec, and took a walk down memory lane. We spent a night in the very lodge we had gone to for three weeks every summer as a family. Then we toured the Island, rented bikes, stayed in a variety of bed and breakfast places, ate ice-cream cones, and reminisced on this beautiful, peaceful Island. It seemed almost the same as it was all those many years ago. For about four days I savored the healing powers of the ocean, family memories, and having these stolen moments as sisters. Looking back, I wondered what I was hoping to find there.

Some might hear this story and think, "She must have had a nervous breakdown to do such a rash thing." In fact, that is what some people did say. Others, who perhaps have shared a similar moment of clarity, would read this and know it was a moment when I was one hundred per cent in tune with my soul.

Was this an act of self-love or one of desperation? Was it driven by courage or fear? To me, this was a moment of clarity when my soul spoke up from within and said, "You must find a way to be true to yourself. You must find a way to start your journey to an authentic life." How does one do that when there is no blueprint or guidelines? Clearly, I needed help.

Looking back, I cannot believe that I did this. What snapped inside me, and/or what came together, to enable me to get in my car without any plan and undertake that thirteen-hour drive? Never once, in over thirty years, had I set out on my own before. And then to leave my car at my daughter's and fly across the country to my sister's home in Toronto! I don't remember the details of how this trip to Prince Edward Island was coordinated so quickly or how my sister was able to get away from their family business on such short notice. I remember the travel agent telling me these things needed to be planned months in advance if you were travelling in the summer, which we were. The travel agent couldn't know that I had the Universe working in the background making the impossible possible.

Even when we know that a change is becoming mandatory, how do we then let go of everything that has made sense up until that moment? When we have invested so much of our time, energy, and commitment, driven by our values, into something that no longer works for us, where do we find the tools and the strength to begin a new life? Transformation is never optional, empowerment will only happen with baby steps, and renewal will surprise us.

What is your truth will not be every person's truth. My mind took me back to one of my dad's favorite quotes, one that he used to share when he spoke of alcoholics on their road to recovery and sobriety: "If a man does not keep pace with his companions, perhaps it is because he hears a different drummer. Let him step to the music which he hears, however measured or far away."[6] I knew I had crossed the line for many of my friends and extended family, and many would not be able to understand what I was doing and why, but I needed to "step to the music" I was hearing.

My music inside had gone silent. I could no longer serve two "masters." There was a bubbling volcano of emotions inside begging me to be kind to my own self, and I could no longer find any semblance of calm in my heart. I was not able to push myself to accept a family that no longer mirrored the vision I had of family. Of course I did not process any of this at the time. I just knew I could not stay. The how, the where, the why would all have to evolve. I had to believe that what my new family would look like would somehow be far more beautiful.

This seemingly sudden "breaking point," or disconnect with one's status quo, is not limited to a broken relationship. It can happen if a career has gone off the rails, a health issue changes one's options for the future, a financial disaster results in bankruptcy, a dream to have children is lost forever, and many other things. How we respond is greatly influenced by how well we are able to continue to love ourselves through it all. Our non-linear world touches every life, and we can never know when it will be our turn to do the work of listening to our soul. Tracking the insights I learned through the process from each transformation to renewal has given me the confidence to believe in my abilities and own who I am becoming.

I asked the Universe, "How will I get to the other side? How will I ever come to accept what is, what was, and what will never be? What can I find to replace what is lost? How will I ever feel whole again?" Eventually, it was me that answered these questions—with the help of an incredible counselor and many wonderful authors. I was guided to understand that everything I needed was inside me. It would take work, time, courage, and love.

The special art of being a successful counselor is knowing what questions to ask. They may make a comment or offer a new perspective at

---

6 Henry David Thoreau, *Oxford Essential Quotations*, 5th ed. (Oxford University Press, 2017), https://www.oxfordreference.com/display/10.1093/acref/9780191843730.001.0001/q-oro-ed5-00010905 .

the very time you are open to hearing it. Sometimes even a friend or an acquaintance can make a simple observation that stirs one's soul. We cannot be told to listen to our soul, but we can feel that little nudge inside that beckons us to take a new step in a different direction. Baby steps lead to giant ones.

There have been many books that "found me" at different times in my healing journey. It would be impossible to single out all the special messages I felt were written just for me. Books came into my life in a variety of ways; some were gifts and others were ones I found while looking for presents for other people. Sometimes people who crossed my path recommended books. Throughout the years, I also gravitated to books whose title or a chapter resonated in my heart.

If you go on this quest and make a list of books that you have read throughout the years, this list can sometimes look like "passages" of your life and help you to understand yourself and your journey better. I definitely recommend that you pay attention to the books that you may hear about unexpectedly. It can be surprising how perfectly timed that very book could be in your life. If you think like I do, you will believe that "Someone" sent that book to you at just that moment in your life.

One of the most memorable messages for me can be found at the beginning of *The Invitation* and it touched my soul forever. This powerful phrase that follows is from Oriah Mountain Dreamer's much-loved poem that explores how vulnerable we are prepared to be on the road to self-discovery and authenticity: "I want to know if you can disappoint another to be true to yourself; if you can bear the accusation of betrayal and not betray your own soul."[7] This is exactly what I was feeling as I made my trip across Canada and spent time on Prince Edward Island with my sister. My trip across the country had far surpassed what I ever could have imagined I would do to honor the longings of my heart.

I asked myself, "How did two people drift so far apart after years of building a great family life?" It is simple, really. It is the souls that lose their connection, gradually, over time. If two people value life in significantly

---

7 Oriah, *The Invitation* (San Francisco: HarperSanFrancisco, 1999)

different ways, these differences eventually create a separation of hearts that cannot be repaired. Feelings deep in one's mind, body, and soul have power. No one "sees" them and no one but you can appreciate or anticipate the wear and tear that these feelings can cause. One day, it is simply not working anymore. Years of spiritual isolation have combined to sever the connection between these two souls. It is as if the soul finally finds its voice after a deep, dark, long journey when it struggled to try to deny its own truth. Then, all of a sudden, that same soul finds its voice and is ready to make the necessary changes.

One day, that soul may find itself in a car driving away from its life hoping to find a better one. With the help of a wonderful counselor, I was able to believe that healing was possible and begin the journey to a new life with possibilities I never could have imagined.

Insights to Own Who You Are Becoming –
Connecting with Your Inner Voice

There has been so much research done in recent years on the brain, and it is remarkable to know that it can be rewired at any time to create new possibilities in our lives. But have we discovered how to get more closely synchronized with what our souls need? Can you think of a time when your soul took over and demanded your attention? Did it find its way into your heart with a song, a book, a speaker, a movie or a dear friend? Was it shocking, or did you already know that you were not meeting your deepest needs to become your authentic self?

It has been written that if you want tomorrow to be different from yesterday, you need to do something different today. What does "something different" look like for you? How can you make that easier to pursue? What would a first step to "something different" require? Would it be driven by reason or passion? In the quote that opens this chapter, Kahlil Gibran suggests that the soul needs both in order to sing![8] Would your next step make sense to anyone else, or even to you? In our quest to be true to ourselves, we need to find ways to honor who we are, even if our daily commitments demand that we compromise who we really are in the present moment.

Souls can lose connections with each other, but the real risk to our happiness is when we lose the path to our own soul. This is the power of denial, when we simply reject the facts in order to fit our lives into the story we are telling ourselves. Is there some deep truth inside you that you need help with so you can safely integrate it into your daily life? Is there a way to face your truth and at the same time protect your soul? Authenticity on this level is where a qualified counselor could make a great difference. Brainstorm an action plan to become more in tune with the needs of your soul and release its energy into your life. Find ways to give yourself permission to own and honor your deepest needs.

---

8 Kahil Gibran, "On Reason and Passion," Poets.org, Academy of American Poets, https://poets.org/poem/reason-and-passion .

Notes to Own Who You Are Becoming:

_____

_____

_____

_____

_____

_____

_____

_____

_____

_____

_____

_____

_____

_____

Chapter 4

What If It Is Possible to Heal?

Only that day dawns to which we are awake. There is more day to dawn.
The sun is but a morning star.

—Henry David Thoreau (1817-1862), *Walden*
American Naturalist, Essayist, Poet & Philosopher

IN LESS THAN A MONTH after I returned home from my two-week trip across Canada, I had literally stepped back into the exact role and life I had left. How does this happen? Why didn't someone step in and say, "Wait a minute. There is a real problem here. We need to address it and repair these lives in whatever way we can." The fact is, "that someone" was not strong enough or healed enough to know what should happen next. In fact, there was no one in the family or the extended family strong enough emotionally to imagine and/or suggest what a next step might look like.

Did I think I could go to Prince Edward Island with my sister, capture the wonderful feelings of being young and carefree, and heal enough to find the strength to go back to my "real" life? I even missed my youngest daughter's twenty-third birthday, a memory that still makes me sad. Birthdays were always, and still are, a very special day to be remembered and celebrated by all the family. Whatever possessed me? And now, I had slipped into "business as usual," coping with my life one day at a time, in the only way I knew how.

When one's heart is broken and one's soul has lost its way, one is unable to think clearly; however, one cannot just take a break from their life and then "go back." To make it possible to heal, the wounded heart will need to value the outcome enough to risk the necessary steps to get there. It will require them to create a paradigm shift in how they see their role in life and depend on how deeply self-love can support them.

Many are familiar with the phrase "there is an elephant in the room, but no one sees it"; actually, everyone sees it. The reason it fails to cause the onlookers to take action is due to the way they have chosen to perceive it. How we see things is greatly influenced by our personal set of beliefs. Paradigms can create a belief system that is so strong it overrides reality. If you cannot believe you have a right to be happy, even if it means letting other people down, you will not be able to think it is possible to heal.

Many years ago, we showed a video about paradigm shifts to all who attended our career program. It featured ideas presented by Thomas Samuel Kuhn, an American historian and philosopher of science, in his 1962 book *The Structure of Scientific Revolutions*. One story I remember was that if a scientist looks through a microscope and sees something that is contrary to everything they have studied and learned in a book, they may alter what they see in the microscope.[9] They will even change a new truth to match their old concepts in their report. Another term for this is philosophical biases, and much can be found about this on the internet. This is an amazing fact that demonstrates the power of paradigms. Imagine if you put your feelings under a microscope and they looked like someone else's feelings. It is not easy to change what we have spent a lifetime believing, even if it was what we needed to do in order to heal.

There is a delightful story that demonstrates the power of paradigms that touched my heart some years ago. There was a man with six children of all ages on a bus early one Sunday morning. They were running up and down the aisle of the bus, and so the quiet and sparsely occupied ride that all the passengers on board were expecting was anything but quiet. Naturally, some became very annoyed.

---

9 Though I no longer have access to this video, examples of Kuhn's discussion of paradigms and how things are perceived can be seen in Samuel Kuhn, "Revolutions as Changes of World View," *The Structure of Scientific Revolutions*, 3rd ed. (University of Chicago Press, 1996), 111–135.

Then the man said, "I am so sorry for the children's energy this morning and I apologize if they are disturbing you. We have been at the hospital all night and their mother passed away early this morning." Suddenly the passengers' indignant disapprovals of all the noise and unruly behavior and their belief that children should be seen and not heard, shifted to compassion and understanding; they were easily able to make a paradigm shift in their expectations of what was appropriate behavior for the children's behavior on the bus.

However, in my story, we are talking about rethinking a lifetime of beliefs about what a family should be. Since this was clearly not the life I had imagined for myself and my family, I needed to have a massive paradigm shift to give myself permission to leave my marriage. I had grown up believing in the "happily ever after" of marriage and the spiritual values of "till death do us part," and now I would need a complete makeover from the inside out to confront the "elephant in the room" head on.

As I mentioned in the last chapter, for the first time in my life, I agreed to see a counselor, and in that very first appointment, I reached a turning point. Since this was our first meeting, I tried to calmly tell her some of the things I thought were relevant, just as you would tell a doctor your symptoms. I listed a series of recent life events as if I was a reporter summarizing the facts. I heard the counselor quietly say, "This is like a jet plane has crashed over the roof of your home and you don't know where to begin to pick up the pieces."

I shocked myself when I broke down into uncontrollable sobbing. She was the first person in over four years who validated and put into words the magnitude of my losses. I shared that I was not falling apart from the past year and all the things that had happened in twelve short months, including the detail that my mom had died recently. I was drowning in denial of so many challenges that grew over the years and deceiving myself that there was no mountain high enough that I could not climb it.

I came to this counselor because I wanted someone to give me an objective opinion on what I should do with my life and my marriage. Of course, like so many of us, I already had an idea and wanted her to agree with it. I told her that I was working through the choice to stay in this marriage of thirty-two years or to leave. I was sure my decision to stay was the best one.

There were six lives to consider and if one, me, could just suck it up, settle, and live the second half of her life in a silent state of sadness, the other five people could be precluded from having to go on the painful journey of separation.

As I put into words the exact thinking for my decision, which at the time I thought made perfect sense, it is surprising that the counselor didn't just burst out laughing or have some other equally strong reaction. No, my counselor was a wonderful professional. She listened quietly, and then she replied with a response that will forever resonate with me. She said, "There are no free rides here. Whatever you choose, your decision is a lesson of love for your children for all of their future days. What would you say to them thirty years from now if they were in an unhealthy relationship? Would you wish that you had left your marriage because you wanted them to now do the same and regret that it was too late to set the example?"

Wow! I sat there thinking of the person I wanted to be in the lives of my children, then and forever. I wanted my children to grow up trusting in life, to know what courage can achieve, to learn the power of hope, and that if we can believe before we can see, we can take ourselves on a journey to a better life and a better place within our own soul. I also knew there would always be friends and family who would never understand; I had to remind myself they were not walking in my shoes. They would observe my actions, but the tsunami of my feelings could never be put into words.

I left my appointment with the counselor knowing that I had a mountain to climb, but it was now a mountain that I was choosing to climb; I now understood why, and for some unknown reason it felt that somehow we would all be OK. I was at peace.

I had never wanted to be labelled "divorced," and I had always hoped for a love that could last forever. We often convince ourselves that it's best for everyone if we just carry on and silently bear the suffering. However, this paradigm shift allowed me to see that it was not only possible to seek healing, but this decision would be beneficial for everyone in the long run. I could define my own label to myself. I was not quitting; I was letting go of a lost dream to find a better dream. I finally understood that as we grow to own who we are becoming, we can give positive meanings to personal choices that once only felt negative. Loving ourselves makes this possible.

Throughout the process of letting go of the image of the family I had had hoped we would be, I sought out the wisdom of some of my inspiring heroes and authors. I came across the book *Life Beyond Measure: Letters to My Great-Granddaughter* by Sidney Poitier, one of my all-time favorite people. It inspired me to want to share the decision-making process behind my leaving my marriage with my fifteen-year-old granddaughter. She had asked me to tell her about a difficult decision I had to make and how I was able to do it. I share it with you now; perhaps there may be something that you can relate to as well.

To my beautiful granddaughter: Celebrate all your brave decisions. At fifteen, it is wonderful to know you can reach inside and own who you are and what you need. You will always be your greatest critic. Your standards will always be harsher than those who love you. The challenge after each personal decision is to "own it." Own who you are, why you made your decision, and move on. To step back, even for a brief minute or two, and second guess what you decided and the action that followed is to undermine the greatness of your commitment to decide for yourself. Every choice we make with our gift of free will and our mind makes it possible for each of us to weigh the pros and cons, the yin and yang of every decision. We can calculate what a best choice is for us and why with the knowledge and experience we have gleaned throughout our life. Each path we take becomes a building block with a life lesson for the next choice. When I made the decision to leave my marriage my core value of family and marriage was in direct conflict with my core value to be true to myself, and equally important, to be the living example of courage to my children. I looked to the words of Eleanor Roosevelt:

> *You gain strength, courage and confidence by every experience in which you really stop to look fear in the face. You are able to say to yourself, "I have lived through this horror. I can take the next thing that comes along . . . . You must do the thing you think you cannot do."*[10]

---

10 Eleanor Roosevelt, *You Learn by Living: Eleven Keys for a More Fulfilling Life* (Louisville: Westminster John Know Press, 1960), 29–30.

It would be many more months before I could embrace this message and be this example of courage and determination, finding my purpose and push through my fears in what felt like a cruel and uncertain world at the time. I wish you the courage to always embrace you and own who you are and allow your great mind to find your many purposes in the journey of life. You have so much to offer the world and you will continue to have even more over the years ahead. With Love and Gratitude, Grandma

So how does one begin the journey to healing and embracing paradigm shifts? I sought the wisdom of gifted writers who shared their thoughts on loving our lives through the challenges. When my four children were young and I had very little time to call my own I found a wonderful book called, *Living, Loving & Learning*. My children were very close in age and I was trying to balance my dedication to them and my need for some "me" time.

The author of this book, Leo F. Buscaglia, was promoting the message that loving really must start within ourselves; he shared that the more we take time for ourselves to grow, the more we will have to offer those we love.[11] This helped me to seek a better balance and not feel guilty when I spent time away from my children to care for myself. It seems that we will never really be done learning this lesson to take time to love ourselves and respond to our needs; it is too easy to slip back. It also takes work and constant reminders. However, the results of this work are always worth it.

Could we start by changing the question that turns the title of this chapter into a confident statement? "It is possible to heal." First, we have to confront the magnitude of the dragon. We have to understand that its power can largely be found in our paradigms. To heal we will need to change our frame of reference and accept that love may not be forever; to get to an authentic place for ourselves and all of our loved ones we may need to redefine the image of a loving family. There will be times when, in order to be true to all of our values, we will need to accept the fact that it may have to impact others' lives and we may be required to let go of deeply held paradigms. Letting go of "happily ever after" is a big one. When one

---

11 Leo F. Buscaglia, *Living Loving & Learning* (New York, Ballantine Books, 1982).

signs up for marriage, no matter the number of ones we know statistically will fail, we hope ours will last forever; in fact, we are counting on it. But many realize, like me, that even if it might make life difficult for themselves and their family, leaving that so-called "happily ever after" can be needed to find true happiness.

Healing is a process and loving is a journey. They both require courage and a willingness to accept the things we cannot change and a willingness to change the things we can, just like the Serenity Prayer guides us to do. [12]

There are no winners in divorce. There is an emotional and financial loss and the feeling of personal failure that no one can escape. As we find ourselves reliving conversations and rethinking decisions, many years later, our fragile hearts beg us to let go. It is done. This process makes me think of the quote in the introduction of my book from Rainer Maria Rilke: "Perhaps then you will gradually, without noticing it, live along some distant day into the answer."[13] In that moment of my life, I knew I had to live my questions. "What if it is possible to heal?" What if we can all live a happier life apart? What if we can create a new paradigm, a new set of beliefs about what a family could be and discover how we could still all love and support each other? What if divorce is a fact of life and not intended to define us? What if there are gifts in new beginnings, even if one of them is divorce or in fact any breakdown of a relationship? What if the decision to respond to the needs of our soul is our finest hour?

Magically, one day when I was sorting through things, I found a special notebook that my dad kept to collect thoughts about life. He would be 107 today. The title of this list was "Great Words of Our Time". It felt as if he was with me contributing to similar sentiments I had written in my book. It was also amazing to realize that without knowing it prior to him passing away, we were soulmates, as we both had a love of inspiring quotes and the

---

12 Reinhold Niebuhr, "Serenity Prayer," Alcoholics Anonymous, February 2024, https://www.alcoholics-anonymous.org.uk/magazines/the-serenity-prayer/ .

13 Rainer Maria Rilke, *Letters to a Young Poet*, Translation by M. D. Herter Norton (New York: W.W. Norton and Company, 1954), 35.

desire to combine many of them in a journal that often blended in with our own original thoughts.

The following special message I found touched me even as I struggled to find peace of mind after my divorce. He quoted from the book Love is Letting Go of Fear: "Peace of mind is our single goal. Through forgiveness, we can learn not to judge others and to see everyone, including ourselves, as guiltless. We can let go of fear when we stop projecting the past into the future and live only in the now."[14]

By focusing our energy on one day at a time, we can find it easier to believe that healing is possible and shift our thinking to the power of hope, something we may have lost in the depths of our sadness. I learned over the years that one of the best ways to recover hope is to embrace the powerful message from the mantra "Just for Today" (first attributed to Frank Crane by some sources but now used widely by AA); it is a wonderful philosophy to manage any painful challenges, teaching us that life is easier one day at a time. It contains a beautiful guide with concrete things we can do each day that will empower us to find ways in our daily routine to heal.[15]

Our biggest lesson in owning who we are becoming and moving beyond each ending toward subsequent new beginnings is to remember to love ourselves through it all. I was grateful that a qualified counselor came into my life to show me that if I wanted to be able to freely love my children, I had to start with myself. No matter how dramatic and soul-destroying change can feel, it is possible to heal. Healing is not only our right, it is our responsibility, and it requires daily attention. We must take the time to find ways to listen to our soul and connect to our inner voice so we can understand the depth of our needs. This is a foundational process in our journey to successfully transform our lives. Slowly, with baby steps, I found my voice, and I share how in the next chapter.

---

14 Gerald G. Jampolsky, *Love is Letting Go of Fear*, 3rd ed. (California: Celestial Arts, 2011), 32.

15 Frank Crane, "Dr. Crane Says," *Boston Globe*, 1921, quoted in quote research, "Just for Today, I Will Try to Live Through This Day Only" Quote Investigator, July 26, 2012, https://quoteinvestigator.com/2012/07/26/just-for-today/#google_vignette .

Insights to Own Who You Are Becoming – Shifting to the Power of Hope

Think of a time, even as a small child, when you might have fantasized and tried to create a reality inside your mind. Over the years, we usually discover that our actual life is often not what others see on the outside. In our self-esteem workshop in the career program that I taught, we often talked about one's "secret self" and one's "social self." Understanding your "secret self" can be a way to truly know yourself and choose when to be authentic in your outer world. It is one's "secret self" that is often in conflict with one's own value system, as I was about my marriage. To know you cannot let your life stay the same when, in the eyes of the world, you seem happy, requires a paradigm shift and a leap of faith. It is an important step in our path to healing.

Was there a time when you had to take the necessary steps to create a new life? Was there someone who guided you to your inner truths? If the new beginning is dramatic, it is rare for us to get to the other side and reality by ourselves.

I believe that denial is both a powerful survival tool and a paradigm entrenched in a belief system we can't get past. We can get stuck in the thinking that the devil we know is better than the devil we don't know. However, life demands that we proceed without knowing if it will all work out in so many areas: will the business thrive, will my children grow up strong and successful, will my marriage be a happy one, will I succeed at this new career, will I be accepted for who I truly am, and so many more unanswered questions plague us. But each time we dare to step out into the dark unknown and things go better than we thought, we reach a new level of optimism. We can build on the positive moments of each new beginning to make the next one easier, and we are often able to embrace it sooner. The power of hope within us is earned and strengthened every time we risk making a change and successfully survive and even thrive in the transformation.

It is important to ask for help, even as we tell ourselves we can climb the mountain alone. Although family and friends are always willing to help us, sometimes a counselor or coach can guide us to our own answers just by listening. We not only see them as a neutral sounding board, but a safe

41

one who, by design, is not going to judge any of our thoughts. They are trained to ask the best questions to help us find our own truths deep within our soul. This is an important step to own who we are becoming. Is there someone you could reach out to that could help you move forward?

Write out a list of things you love (or perhaps used to love before you became sad and defeated) and commit to doing one each day. Is it music, exercise, journaling, baking, running, walking in nature, reading, drawing, or coffee with a friend? Seek out a power greater than yourself, either a professional counselor and/or a spiritual one. These are all small ways to touch your soul with the incredible power of hope and use it in your quest to make healing possible. What would have to happen for you to have even a slight glimmer of hope in your current situation? Wake up to what is possible in this moment, take baby steps, and let the power of hope guide you. Believe you can heal and you will. It will take time.

Chapter 5

From Sadness in Silence to Salvation

Though no one can go back and make a brand new start
Anyone can start from now and make a brand new ending.

—Carl Bard (AKA Carl Sandburg) (1886-1953)
American Writer and Editor, Two Time Pulitzer Prize Winner

IT HAD NOW BEEN SEVERAL months since the life changing appointment with the counselor in which I had come to terms with my decision to leave my marriage. I thought about the story we used to share in the career program about the five frogs sitting on a lily pad. Three of them decided to jump off. Then how many were left on the lily pad? The answer is five. Three of them only "decided" to jump off, they didn't actually do it. So here I was processing what needed to happen to get me "off the lily pad" on the path to a new life, scary as it was to imagine.

This is the moment of truth in one's quest to transform: can you collaborate with your mind, body and soul? Remember, transformation is never optional. The direction we take is guided by believing that it is possible to heal and embracing the power of hope to energize the steps needed to take action. Had I reached that level of courage to move from silence to salvation? I had shared openly that I could not stay in my marriage and met with a counselor; but then I had all but resumed my life as if nothing had changed.

Early in the fall after my trip to Prince Edward Island, I had attended a training course and started a new job, knowing I would need to support myself now, and no one at my work even knew there was anything wrong in my personal life. My two youngest children were still living at home with us, and we were maintaining a level of respect for everyone, often eating our dinners together when people's schedules coincided, all the while knowing this was temporary.

I was on an extremely big learning curve with my new career and often worked long hours into the night preparing workshop material for the next day. My husband, who was no longer working, continued to busy himself with friends who were also unemployed and/or had flexible hours. However, now that the Christmas season was upon us, the challenges were becoming magnified. I will share a few stories and thoughts during the holiday season to show how I moved forward to navigate this transformation in my life.

An overwhelming sadness was concealed deep in my heavy heart, and fleeting moments of reality made me uncertain. I caught myself thinking, If only . . . Could we still . . . Is it really too late? I knew this was going to be the last of our family Christmases as we had known them for thirty-two years, twenty-six of those years happening in our current home. I was tormented with questions for which there were no answers in the moment; how would I ever get to the other side, to a new start? How would all my children, who were my whole life? How would my husband? I even had concerns for the family dog!

Every family has milestone memories of sadness and loss at Christmas time—we had faced the first one without a beloved grandparent, the one where their mom was literally too sick to get out of bed, the cancer diagnosis when the mom's heart was trying to push away the fear she might not see another Christmas with her children, the year the paramedics brought Grandma home from the hospital just for one day and one night, as it would for sure be her last Christmas, the first Christmas that one of the children would not be able to come home, and the Christmas they had just received a guilty verdict.

This Christmas, on the surface, seemed to have all our same cherished Christmas traditions: opening stockings in the living room (which even Lucky, the family dog, was allowed to join!) followed by a decadent breakfast, then entering the magical setting of the family room with all its Christmas lights, children delivering presents to each other, and gift opening, accompanied by all the squeals of delight of the children. Looking back, I felt that even the creators of Disney stories would be hard pressed to depict a more magical family Christmas scene. My fondest memory is how each of my four children, from a very young age, were *almost* more excited to see if the lucky recipients they had bought gifts for loved their present as much as they hoped they would.

You may ask, how did this façade of a last Christmas happen? Well, the overwhelming pain of any lost dream is something we want to avoid at all costs, so we humans have found ways to deny our reality until we are now on the edge of a cliff and sometimes even close to self-destruction. This power to alter how our hearts are experiencing life can be a temporary gift and buy us time. We convince ourselves it's just easier not jumping off the lily pad for now, even though the plan is to take that leap someday.

Many books have been written about the power of our mind's ability to deny, live through, and overcome the unimaginable. One of the greatest examples of this is how, in spite of what Holocaust survivors went through, much worse than what most of us face, many of their stories give powerful examples of what the human spirit can endure. Many shared how they went on to find deep meaning in life and a way to forgive others and love themselves and their life again. One of the most profound examples is told by Viktor E. Frankl in *Man's Search for Meaning*. In this book he writes, "When we are no longer able to change a situation, we are challenged to change ourselves."[16]

In times of great despair, we may try to tap into this power and deny our reality; it may appear to be much easier than initiating change. However, this can work against us when we want the dream so badly we proceed to live as if it is still possible when it is not. If our energy then becomes focused on how to keep the dream alive, we may lose hope and no longer be able to believe in a new dream.

Another barrier to moving forward happens when we allow ourselves to be influenced, even manipulated, sometimes knowingly and sometimes

---

16 Viktor E. Frankl, *Man's Search for Meaning*, translated by Ilse Lasch, (Boston: Beacon Press, 1946)

not, when a person in our lives is living "as if" everything is fine when it is not. They can be so good with the dismissive words and actions that "cover up" your mutual reality that it can create self-doubt and impact your resolve to create a new beginning. This can happen in any codependent relationship, such as in a family dealing with alcoholism, a violent marriage, an abusive childhood, or with an addict. It can be very destructive. You can actually come to think that maybe you were wrong and what you thought you knew to be true may not be.

The road ahead after a lost dream is scary, so much so that many never take it. We resist fixing what we know is broken, even when we know we have lost a piece of the puzzle and it will never be found. The dream as we knew it is gone. However, we tell ourselves we can carry on without that missing piece. We settle in silence. Why?

Alternatively, we can stay strong and true to our commitment to heal and make today the first day of the rest of our life. Can you decide to trust that there is a new life out there that will not be perfect but still believe that it can become beautiful again, one day at a time? We might need to get more help from a counselor and/or a friend to follow through and start a new chapter in our life.

Life can be a series of new beginnings. It is this acceptance of the lost dream, combined with a deep trust that life can be good again, that makes Henry David Thoreau's quote so powerful: ". . . if one advances confidently in the direction of his [or her] dreams, and endeavors to live the life which he [or she] has imagined, he [or she] will meet with a success unexpected in common hours."[17] It is only when we are willing to take a first step that we can start the process of carving out a new life.

One of the most powerful phrases by Deepak Chopra is "No debt in the Universe ever goes unpaid."[18] This next story shows how karma can jump out and help you believe in life in a way you could never have imagined, just like it did for me after that Christmas when I was feeling so stuck.

---

17 Henry David Thoreau, Forbes Quotes, *Forbes*, retrieved September 16, 2024, https://www.forbes.com/quotes/3980/ .

18 Deepak Chopra, *The Seven Spiritual Laws of Success:, A Practical Guide to the Fulfillment of Your Dreams* (San Rafael, CA: Amber-Allen Publishing, 1994), 45.

Not long after the very emotional last Christmas that led me to seek out more support from the counselor, I was in a bad car accident, a near head-on collision. I blacked out and my car travelled a block uphill full of smoke from the explosion of the two airbags in the front seat before stopping. A total stranger pulled me out of the driver's window and then left me with an "angel" standing on the curb, waiting to help. In that moment I knew that regardless of the sadness and pain, if we are open and paying attention, the days will reveal the subtle but constant ways we are never really the architect of our own destiny and we are never truly alone.

On my lonely road to happier times evidence of the path to salvation came in numerous ways. Miraculously, I was able to walk away from this accident without any physical injuries, but this was not the only unexpected gift that day. It was the first time I had ever purchased "replacement car insurance"; therefore, the relatively newly leased car, which was now deemed a write-off, would be replaced with a brand-new car and I would no longer have any lease payments at a time when I was about to begin life on my own with a limited budget. Not that long before I had used some of my recent inheritance when my mom died to pay cash for a car for my husband after he not only lost his job but also lost the use of a company car. Karma was working overtime that day because now neither of us would have a car payment.

My good Samaritan, who stayed with me until my daughter could come, became a lifelong friend, another "angel" in my difficult journey, and even one who loved Starbucks as much as I did! She arranged to deliver me to my oldest daughter at a nearby Starbucks as my car had to be towed. I could not help but feel in awe of how this experience unfolded.

When I reflected on these events, I was overwhelmed by the ways of the Universe, ways that we can never know in advance. This was an "aha" moment for me that has stayed with me all these years. I will always believe that this horrific car accident, which could have had such a different ending, was a "gift" and "a promise" and "a sign"; Something or Someone out there that I could not see or touch and could only feel and believe, was watching out for me. It left me feeling confident that there would be signs, people and things, to enable me to grow strong again.

One day in the silence of our sadness, we will finally understand the profound truth—transformation is never optional. I knew now that to find a new dream, I must let go of all of the old dream, including everything I cherished about our special family Christmas celebrations. I would need to rebuild it all. Often, we move through our days and we miss the significant signs of a new and beautiful life taking shape. I slowly became ready to take the next step on the road to becoming: empowerment in baby steps.

My wish for you is that you will have many experiences that expand your trust in an unseen Benevolent Source. If you continue to show up, pay attention, trust the process, and let go of the delivery details, believing in a new dream will become easier. Transformation is never optional and it can be a very long process. The outcome of this accident became a gift in the midst of a very difficult new beginning. It fueled my belief that if I committed to being active in the steps to a new beginning, I would be empowered to uncover many special dreams. All of this would require that I become more comfortable with the unknown and remember that I am not the sole architect of my own destiny on the road to owning who I am becoming.

Insights to Own Who You Are Becoming –
Believing in a New Dream

Is there a dream you have deep in your heart that you hope you can make come true one day? Have you already gone through the process of watching a dream slowly dissolve? Were you blindsided when you suddenly lost a dream? Did you try to fight to keep your dream alive, only to realize you could not succeed? Are you in the middle of the struggle now dealing with the ambivalence of letting go or holding on? Everything has an end date; how can you become stronger with each one?

Losing a dream is a long, lonely road; it doesn't usually happen overnight. Think of something you might be grieving over and feel you have lost. It could be a divorce, but it could be any life-changing event when you are called upon to recreate yourself and let go of the "you" and your life as you had known it and/or imagined it could be. Accidents, illness, death, career changes, and decisions around having children are just some of the things one may need to work through in sadness and silence. Salvation can come, but each ending requires a new beginning; our potential for success is dependent on the voice inside us that says, "I will believe before I can see and I will start by believing in myself." In fact, we can add another voice to that: "I will own who I am becoming and I will make it my life's work." How can you start this process? Remember there are resources that can help you, such as professional counseling and safe friends and family.

Salvation requires us to get comfortable with not knowing the how or when in every single new beginning. It demands that we stay in the "now" and find quiet moments to reflect on what we can do in this very moment. What step can you take today to begin as if you already know you will be OK? Find your voice even if you are only talking to yourself. Expect that there will be gifts to lift your spirits and support you in setbacks and ongoing feelings of doubt. Create an arsenal of "karma moments," however tiny and insignificant they seemed at the time.

Believing in a new dream is the start of one's salvation. It is the spark to light the fire inside your soul that allows you to believe that you will heal and hope will energize you. Find one to sustain you through today, even if it feels impossible. Let your dream sit in your soul to move you from your sadness in silence to your salvation. I came upon this beautiful quote in the midst of my quest to create my own happiness in new beginnings: "Learn to write your hurts in the sand and carve your blessings in stone."[19] Can you list some of your blessings to replace your hurts and begin a new chapter on the way to believing in a new dream?

19 Priya Sher, "Carve Your Blessings in Stone," *Priya Sher's Blog*, June 13, 2011, https://priyafengshuisolutions.wordpress.com/2011/06/13/carve-your-blessings-in-stone/ .

Part 2

Empowerment
In Baby Steps

As one grows stronger through the steps of transformation, one day, it may suddenly seem that we feel stronger than we ever thought possible. Then something happens. Out of the blue, with no apparent reason, we lose that strength of self we thought we had captured forever. It can happen in an instant. If we can learn to recognize how that personal power can be nurtured, we can take charge. We can become intentional and redirect the baby steps to find a pattern of personal empowerment. Each of us is different, and yet, in some important ways, we are all the same. Our souls can lead the way and our stories can be retold with new insights. We can become the observer of our lives and love ourselves back to empowerment. This is an ongoing journey of baby steps throughout our whole lives. We must never stop moving forward, however slowly it might be.

Chapter 6

Tipping Points of Personal Power

You've always had the power . . . .[you] had to learn it for [your]self.

—Glinda the Good Witch, *The Wizard of Oz*,
Directed by Victor Fleming (1889-1949)
American Film Director, Cinematographer & Producer

THERE ARE MANY DIFFERENT TYPES of personal power. Sometimes one's power in communication is clearly defined by one's title or role, but there are many things that affect our personal power and how we see (or do not see) it. In this chapter, we are considering the most important aspects of power for us personally, regardless of our position. It is a strength that we need to grow in order to achieve the best possible feelings of self-worth. The stories we tell ourselves are not always totally factual and they may affect what and who we believe we can control. Personal empowerment is a process often achieved over a lifetime through baby steps and often through trial and error.

Throughout one's life, coming into one's personal power is not always a timely process. It is not even consistent, nor does it grow proportionately with our efforts and/or our desire to be brave. It is so complex that we may not even be aware that we have abandoned ourselves and our right to be real and ask for what we need. When we are living our life, day by day, we are not the observer of our actions, but we could be. We can feel our power if we believe our personal choices are driving our responses.

Alice Walker reminds us that "the most common way people give up their power is by thinking they don't have any."[20] This becomes a critical dynamic when one does not feel safe enough to say what they are thinking, and it causes the communication to be one way. When the soul doesn't feel valued, it slowly shuts down. This can often happen due to depression, being in a toxic relationship, facing structural discrimination, or dealing with many other kinds of hardships. This can become a very final stage in a relationship setting unless one can hold on to their power inside.

When I think back to the relationship I developed with my own personal power throughout the years, my first memory of it involves my father. He was a peaceful, spiritual, kind man, and I always knew he loved me. I grew with him in his journey through rehabilitation in thirty-two years with AA. The childhood memories were never of seeing my father drunk; the recollections I have are of the devastating impact when he lost his temper on a seemingly insignificant issue or alternatively withdrew into a deep depression and became emotionally unavailable to anyone else in our family. It left me with a permanent takeaway that "keeping the peace" was the best approach no matter what I was thinking or what I wanted to say out loud. Make no mistake, what we learn in our childhood is not easy to modify later on in life, even when we grow up and finally understand the reasons for our choices.

Many people have listed qualities about the middle child and just as many others believe what has been documented has no scientific foundation. However I, as the middle child, definitely fit into the mold of one often stated characteristic, namely that of "peacemaker." I also learned this well from my wonderful mother, who spent a lifetime trying to compensate for the unpredictable emotional rollercoaster we were always riding due to my dad's bouts of depression. We never discussed this as a family, which would have been so valuable at the time. She was also a "middle child."

Over the years, when we found ourselves in stressful situations with family, my older sister would often whisper to me, "Don't speak!" She was much better at this than I was, and we would laugh about it later and

---

20 Alice Walker, American Novelist and Short Story Writer, https://www.goodreads. com/quotes/15083-the-most-common-way-people-give-up-their-power-is

54

review how things had escalated—often, she thought, due to my daring to offer an enthusiastic opinion. This strategy to apply the idea that silence is one of the hardest arguments to refute, and perhaps the best way to keep a semblance of peace, can sometimes be a form of personal power. However, it also removes the opportunity to open up a dialogue that has the potential to result in a better understanding between two people. We sometimes hear people say that we should "pick our battles," and this is good advice when we are already sure the parties involved are too far apart in their thinking to find any common ground. Although silence can definitely limit our ability to be transparent, share our thoughts, and resolve any differences, we have still exercised our personal power with our choice to remain quiet. The important thing to remember is that personal power is not the same as conflict resolution; the latter requires completely different skills. In addition, it often needs the experience of a qualified mediator.

Silence can carry its own strength when you believe with all your heart that your thoughts matter and they are right for you. However, it takes a very strong person to be comfortable with this type of interaction—staying silent in one's own power even when facing disrespect—without it dramatically impacting their self-esteem. In the absence of honest dialogue with another, it is even more important to connect with your inner voice and stay true to what matters to you. In this instance, you have simply chosen to avoid a verbal conflict, but you have not given up your power and equally important, your commitment to own who you are becoming.

There are so many people with whom we all need to communicate: parents, siblings, employers, committee members, service people, neighbors, extended family members and more. Think about your approach to conflict and how you have dealt with criticism and/or upset people through the years. Ask yourself how you can honor your right to equal personal power and at the same time keep the interactions positive and productive.

Sometimes, when we do try to find our voice and exercise our personal power, other people, even those close to us, may try to shut it down again. As I write now, my mind drifts back to one of our family's weekly routines around chores. My husband oversaw all the outside chores for the children and he would decide in any given week what needed to be done and when. It wouldn't matter to him if anyone had a major exam or assignment the next day. If he thought it might rain and/or it coincided with his schedule, they had to step up and take the hour to two hours to get our very large lawn cut, raked and bagged, or complete all the weeding of an equally big area along the driveway or whatever else he deemed as essential on that day.

I remember one time I quietly risked saying, "Do you think only three of the children could help with the lawn tonight?", since the fourth one had an exam the next day. He quickly replied: "We only need one major general." I thought then, and many times since, that no one else I knew would ever use that analogy to describe me, given my years of actively being a peacemaker. Words can be difficult to erase and this "label" stayed with me for a long time.

You may be reading this little anecdote and thinking, "That is no big deal!" This is where the tone, the words, and the body language combine to influence how a message is received; deep inside, a soul is instinctively responding to the emotions resulting not only from the message, but also from whom it was delivered and how. I had made a reasonable request on behalf of one of my children, and it should have been easy to reach a compromise. Instead, I was left feeling as if I was interfering and was now at fault for increasing the tension. I regretted that sharing a concern or request could not be met with a more respectful response between two parents.

Herein lies the importance of being able to fully understand if there is truth in the words directed at you. Sometimes you may need a confidant of some sort to help you appreciate that your feelings are valid. I also could have chosen to share later with my husband how that response made me feel and it might have been an opportunity to find common ground.

We learn that people have the capacity to trigger our feelings of inadequacy simply by virtue of their defined role; spouses/partners, parents, siblings, and employers are possibly the top four. We expect them to know what we need, but more often they don't. It is up to us to find our voice and dare to share when they upset us; otherwise, how can we expect to achieve any common understanding?

I also remember the year my husband said, in the midst of my two years of cancer treatments, "We don't need any more of these silly sayings hanging on the walls." This collection of décors with inspiring quotes, which inspired me to reach the finish line of my fifty-four cancer treatments, was, in fact, significant. Extended family, my children, and I had all found countless incredible quotes and messages of hope and positivity on beautiful artistic backgrounds. So to be fair, we did have a lot of these hanging up throughout our home.

With or without the immediate need for continuous hope, these "silly sayings" and quotes about courage and positivity are the essence of who I am. Throughout the career program I taught, they called me the "queen of quotes." Remember too, in chapter one, I referenced what might have been the first of my "collections" called Odz 'n Enz by Robert Parsons. I had printed my name in it with my address and phone number, and based on its publication date I must have been about ten years old. Based on the summary that was written in the brief foreword, they were confident that people everywhere, with every kind of human need, would find their lives enriched from the collection of messages of hope written in poetry and prose. [21] Let's face it, my poor husband never stood a chance on changing me; the passion began before I even knew what it was, around the age of ten.

These are little anecdotes with a big message that took me years to fully appreciate. In any relationship, the ideal is a mutual respect of what matters to the other person. They don't have to like the same things or understand why you do. However, for love to thrive, you need to know they love and accept all of who you are without judgment.

These are also very simple stories of how subtle and seemingly innocent verbal abuse can be. When anyone, especially someone close to you, belittles the value of something you love and cherish, it can feel like an attack deep within your soul. Similarly, if you loved flowers or music and they were not permitted in your home, this would create a potentially irreparable break line in the harmony. It might not be a deal breaker, but you would need to seek other kindred spirits who shared these values to validate the essence of who you are.

---

21 Walter L. Wilson, foreword to *Odz 'n Enz*, edited by Robert Parsons (Chicago: Moody Press, 1954), 5.

I believe the mind, body, and soul are always at work together, and I think that they take turns being in charge. Sometimes we are governed by the logic of our emotions, other times our body reacts, and always our soul is keeping score in the background. When we continue to silence our voice, we risk our soul shutting down and, tragically, it is then often too late to find any common ground.

I remember going into a government office for some documents that I needed for my divorce. The clerk, a total stranger, almost like an "angel of enlightenment," volunteered her opinion. I also sensed she was speaking from personal experience. She said, "Verbal abuse can be far more devastating and permanent than physical abuse. This is because no one else can see the continuous wounds to your soul and the scars can last forever. You alone must bear your feelings, and only you are impacted by the words."

I thought as she spoke, it can be confusing to others because the person perpetrating the abuse "hears" the words, but you "feel" the words and are also impacted by the way they were delivered to you and by whom. Memory tends to hold on to hurtful words with a recall like a song; it can take you back to the exact date, time and scenario in which they were said.

As I drove home from the government office I thought about this wonderful quote: "No one can make you feel inferior without your consent."[22] Why don't we simply speak up and state what we need? Why can't we just withhold our permission and refuse to "feel inferior?" I think the answer is simple. We have not understood that the person abusing us does not determine our worth. In addition, we may feel inferior, and may need help from a coach or a counselor or close friend to understand that our value is not determined by the ones who treat us badly. Once we learn to take control of the validity of what is said, we will proudly start to own who we are becoming.

Verbal abuse in any relationship is a perceived imbalance of power. The interpretation and the tone influence how the person hears the words; they filter into one's entire being and can build up over time to create lasting wounds deep within one's soul. The message of the quote by Glinda the

---

22 Eleanor Roosevelt, Forbes Quotes, *Forbes*, retrieved September 12, 2024, https://www.forbes.com/quotes/2610/

Good Witch at the opening of this chapter is significant. We all have to be diligent and grow into our power but it is always there, within us, waiting for us to access it. This is a powerful lesson because we must take responsibility and insist that we find our voice, with baby steps. Here are a few of the moments in which I look back and know the truth of the phrase when you are ready to lose, you are ready to win! These stories demonstrate that when I was confident in my own truth, I was able to successfully become my own advocate and override demeaning responses.

Once, as a young mother of four school-aged children, I had been thinking about going back to work to help with all the costs of raising a family and doing my part to contribute to the family finances. I was perfectly happy to enjoy the summer with my children, and there was no yearning to get out of the house. I was a born mother and was passionate about homemaking and doing things with and for my family. However, stresses caused by the many expenses and pressure from my husband to go back to work, like his colleagues' wives had already done, continued to mount. So, when the call came out of the blue to go for an interview that was initiated by a friend, I thought it must be a sign.

I donned one of the few summer dresses I owned, which was a totally "mother of four children" look in a soft pastel cotton. Now wearing the woman I was on my sleeve, a mom and a homemaker, off I went.

I walked into a small office down in the quaint setting of False Creek near Granville Island to what could have been a warm and intimate interview—perfect for who I was. However, the "gatekeeper" and executive coordinator of this small company was the complete antithesis of me. As she stood there in her chic, corporate, black-and-white attire, it was clear from the moment we met that there was an instant disconnect. The older man, who was the owner and creator of the specialized training program I was being interviewed to promote, was more open to diversities and possibilities, like me.

The standout question in the interview from the "strictly business" assistant was, "You do know that selling corporate seminars to CEOs and senior executives is a lot different to selling Tupperware?" (this was something I had led the country in and had done part time while raising my children). She had failed to digest my entire resume and missed the details about my experience travelling across Canada, interacting with senior executives, teaching companies' employees how to use state-of-the-art office equipment for IBM, and other relevant facts.

Often when a person underestimates our potential, it can be the perfect opportunity to stand out. Sometimes confrontational questions like the one above can trigger a "winning response" you never knew you had inside you. When I heard this woman's condescending question, the fight mechanism in the fight/flight response and adrenalin took over in me. I replied politely, although I was clearly insulted and furious inside, "I don't think you are ever really selling a product, I think you are always only selling enthusiasm, and I have never been short on that." I would have liked to add, "That's something I suspect you know nothing about."

You could have heard a pin drop. The owner was not a poker player by any stretch of the imagination, and he raised his eyes, looking over at the stylish woman, and he smiled in delight. As for the chic executive coordinator, well, she had nothing to say. When I was leaving, the owner said, "I think we could make beautiful music together." Who knows what the outcome would have been with another response or no response! Interestingly, sometime after I had been working there, this man signed his recent book for me, "to the Iron Butterfly." Have you ever noticed how someone can describe you in a unique way that you would never have envisioned yourself?

What I know for sure is that we need to be our own advocate, and it needs to be something we "own" with every fiber of our being. It is an important start in reaching one's potential. We must be ready to respond at a moment's notice in case we are blindsided by an outside force bent on challenging the essence of who we are or who we could be. Taking baby steps to gradually increase our skill for being our own advocate will help to maintain and increase our personal power.

In another story about owning who you are and daring to answer with conviction, it was again a question that triggered the powerful response. Two women began an interview with a fragile woman seeking a job for which she had no specialized training. I say "fragile" not because the woman was not well educated and experienced with an outward appearance of poise; it was because inside, her personal life was falling apart all around her. Ironically, she was literally perfect for the role. No one in that room could yet know how perfect.

After a detailed interview and a conversation that appeared to have created a synergy between interviewers and applicant that one might think led them to lean toward offering her the position, the lead owner said, "How will you make up for the fact that you don't have a master's in counseling?"

Again, as in the previous example, this acted as a trigger to enable her to confidently respond with something she believed with all her heart. Drawing on many of the very things happening in this moment in her own life, she answered with total conviction, "I believe I have a master's in life experiences and that will more than make up for it." This answer made her the second choice for the position until the person with the master's in counselling showed her true colors as a "team member" in less than a week on the job. They then called this "second choice" back for what was a job she fit into perfectly, in which she excelled in every way, and the rest is history, as they say. This person was, of course, me! It was for sure one of the most memorable highlights in my journey to find my personal power.

Others will often challenge who we are and question who we think we are. Never let anyone else define you. Sometimes when another has underestimated your commitment to yourself, this becomes a competitive advantage and the tipping point of your personal power in communication. Find the wise words and quotes of special heroes that you can easily relate to and use them to keep you strong in times when people challenge your personal power.

A favorite of mine comes from Alan Cohen. In Cohen's book *I Had It All the Time,* he reinforces this thought when he writes: "Be sure that you are thinking with your own mind and feeling with your own heart."[23] This is our lifetime goal: to own who we are, how we feel, what we need, and what no longer requires validation from anyone else.

Sometimes, when something blindsides us in life, we lose sight of who we truly are. In this chapter, I have taken a walk down memory lane to

---

23 Alan Cohen, *I Had it All the Time: When Self-Improvement Gives Way to Ecstasy* (Hawaii: Alan Cohen Publications, 1995), 85.

remember my strengths. This can be a key baby step to empower ourselves. To successfully own who we are becoming, we are the only ones who need to believe in our abilities and our values. Whatever we are passionate about is important simply because it fuels our spirit.

One of the greatest examples of the benefit of "remembering" happened each time I sat down with a client to compose their resume in the career program. In uncovering many of the things in their life that had brought them to the current moment, in addition to their formal training, we were able to create a powerful summary of everything they had to offer a prospective employer. My favorite moment was when they would receive a final copy and say, "Is that really me?" They were not only proud of their resume; they were thrilled with the person it represented. Journaling to document some of your strengths is a great way to empower yourself on the road to own who you are becoming.

Discovering how great our potential can be is a process of shifting from being broken to having a breakthrough that will be discussed in greater detail in the next chapter.

Insights to Own Who You Are Becoming – Remembering Your Strengths

Think about times when you surprised yourself with a strong response when someone was challenging your ideas. What or who made it possible to ask for what you needed in that moment? How can you make sure that this happens more often? Protect your mindset by remembering your strengths and keeping them safe deep inside on your personal journey to empowerment. No one but you needs to know or understand their value.

It is hard to be consistent in taking care of ourselves. Sometimes a person or a situation makes us more vulnerable in the moment and we look back and feel disappointed that we did not dare to speak up for ourselves. Breathe, be still, listen to your instincts, and own your greatness. Then, quietly take control and respond. It can be the turning point in the relationship and a chance to shift the power to be, at the very least, equal. Your silence can even be a moment of power. You can walk away and know they did not "win." Can you remember a time when you did this and it felt great?

Always remember that no one else's thoughts or opinions of us matter as much as our own. Hold on to your power with the glowing image of your unique self. Let everyone you meet become a teacher from whom you learn more about yourself. Let every interaction help you discover what really matters and what you feel passionate about defending within yourself. Remember your strengths and learn to accept the value of the differences.

Think about recent contentious conversations and identify what you could have said differently or perhaps have withheld; find the lessons for next time. Empowerment is a process, and it happens with baby steps over a lifetime. It can be as simple as using the word "no" more often. Use it all by itself when you can, or try adding "it no longer works for me;" we do not need to explain our thoughts and feelings, especially when we know the receiver will not relate to them. Nothing positive will be achieved, and it will just delay your chosen outcome.

Notes to Own Who You Are Becoming:

Chapter 7

Broken to Breakthrough

When you come to the edge of all the light you have,
And must take a step into the darkness of the unknown,
Faith is knowing one of two things will happen:
There will be something solid for you to stand on,
or you will be taught how to fly.

—Patrick Overton Ph.D., (1948-2024), *The Leaning Tree*
American Educator, Poet, Playwright & Author

EACH MORNING, AS WE PREPARE to greet the day, intellectually we realize that we can only be sure of what is happening in the present moment. However, we put our trust in the law of averages and what has been predictable in the past. In short, we trust that this day will offer a blend of challenges and opportunities and we will be able to navigate through them all. Then one day, as my counselor so aptly described it, "It is as if a jet plane has crashed over the roof of your home and you don't know where to begin to pick up the pieces." The collection of all of our days becomes our life, and "Life is something which happens while we're waiting for something else!"[24]

---

24 Alan Saunders, *Mary Worth*, comic strip, *Calgary Herald* (Calgary, AB), September 1, 1956, Newspapers.com, https://www.newspapers.com/article/calgary-herald-life-happens-waiting/128614057/ .

Metaphorically speaking, if something is broken into large manageable pieces, we may be able to put it back together with glue. However, if it is shattered in a million pieces, there is no option but to accept that it can't be repaired.

Late one afternoon, I received a phone call from my husband that something had happened at work and I needed to come home right away. I only had to hear the tension in his voice to reply, "OK," hang up, and immediately leave my office. I never asked a single question. In my wildest nightmares, nothing could have prepared me for what I was about to hear upon arriving home.

My husband had been accused of a white-collar crime and his entire future, career, and retirement plan was now over. Looking back all these years later, I realize now that sometimes life presents the unimaginable and there is no way to be able to rationally handle the steps required to move forward without serious professional help. If you are diagnosed with cancer, you are immediately surrounded by a medical team. If you are in a car accident, there is a group of police, ambulance drivers, and medical specialists all available to help. That day, standing in the room listening to my husband recount what his day had involved, I am not sure what caused me to respond the way I did.

In my perception of my role as the matriarch, I believed that I needed to be strong and help the entire family to stand united, face whatever the world was about to throw at us, and do some significant damage control in our hearts and minds. The lives of me, my husband, and our four children had just been shattered to pieces. What I could not know then is that we were all faced with a mountain, and to safely navigate our way back to a new "normal," we needed the guidance of experts. So I said, "No one has died, and nothing is terminal; we can recover from this together."

I share this with you, the reader, so that if anything similar happens in your life, you will reach out for professional help right away. It still may not be enough to "glue" your family or yourself back together, but it may minimize the trauma to each person.

Despite what I said, the reality was "something had died" and "something was terminal." Life as we all knew it would never be the same; it was like we had entered a foreign land we had never experienced, and imagining it was too scary. It would be almost four years from this moment before I sought professional assistance and accepted that I may need help climbing this mountain.

So now the jet plane has crashed over your roof, and now there are a million pieces scattered. Where does one start to rebuild, to move from broken to breakthrough, and even believe there will be a way to find a successful new beginning? If one's entire mode of life has been shattered with no warning, it will not be possible to even visualize the decision stepping stones to a new beginning.

Dramatic change is not for the faint-hearted. It could be leaving a job, ending a marriage, recovering from illness or an accident, losing your persona and identity as the world knows you, rebuilding financially after bankruptcy, and more. In all my years as a career coach, I was in awe of the strength of the human spirit in times of devastating challenges. Slowly, it will be possible to heal, and we will shift to the power of hope. However, initially it is OK to feel powerless when the unimaginable happens. This is where a professional counselor or other experienced support system becomes so necessary—such support helps to guide us with strategic questions that enable us to slowly come to accept our new reality. This might be after an event that just happened, or we may be facing issues we have successfully buried for years. When this moment of crisis came for me, I knew all I could focus on was what had to happen in the next hour; I was at the peak of broken.

It took two and a half years to bring the court case to a conclusion of guilty—a verdict we received practically on Christmas Eve. I am so very proud of the courage and actions all my children took to support both of their parents and the love everyone gave to each other. However, as I can now write and read this like someone else's story, I know we never really healed because we never sought professional help as a family and we never talked with each other about how we felt. We simply survived and moved forward. Learn from this story and look after yourself and your loved ones whenever a tragedy or traumatic experience occurs. Seek professional help.

With the help of a counselor, I came to accept that in difficult times, there are no free rides; a choice must always be made. I had accepted that I could not stay in my marriage. However, I was still too fragile to actually leave altogether (as I detailed in an earlier chapter). Leaving was a work in progress, but seeing a counselor created a wonderful opportunity for a breakthrough that only came about after "breaking."

Looking back, if we are paying attention, often our lives reveal a series of "coincidences." Sometimes the ways of the Universe roll out like a carefully crafted movie or book. It is as if the Universe already knew how to best use these life moments and how to get us to the next chapter in our life.

This was dramatically demonstrated after I had just had a one-hour conversation with my sister in Toronto, calling on my cell phone from Vancouver's beautiful Stanley Park. At that time, this was a fifty-dollar cost. We had been talking at length about what the steps would look like to move my life forward. As we came to say goodbye, I asked my sister, "How will I get there?", and she replied with the honest reality that only an older sister might state: "With a lot of pain."

That was already profound, but then came her parting comment, "Promise me you will keep your phone on." I think she might have meant this metaphorically, telling me to stay open to possibilities and not to lose hope in a better tomorrow. Before I had even left the park, a life-changing phone call came with the question: "Are you still interested in the position of career coach?"

I could not have predicted that my life was going to take the downward/ unexpected turns that it did, and moving forward would cause a lot of pain. However, as this phone call shows, life (or the Universe) also often provides unexpected positive turns, which is something to remember when we face moments of "breaking." This laid the foundation for me to begin to trust life again and believe in happy endings.

To trust in the unknown and in our choices as we move through each day is hard. Letting go of the timing of our dreams and the exact details as they unravel takes humility. Who could have known there would be a way to take my heartache and change the direction of my life from broken to breakthrough? Who could have imagined that the Universe already had laid out the perfect next step for me to use my whole life to help and heal others? Certainly not me. All I committed to, at the request of my loving older sister, was staying connected, at the very least by phone, and continuing to believe in possibilities and showing up. This is the most important action when moving toward a new life.

Within three months of that thirteen-hour journey alone by car that I shared in chapter three, I was placed in a job that became the "vehicle" for me to literally take my life, with all its pain and disappointments, and find its purpose. Throughout my role as a career coach to well over a thousand people with diverse professional backgrounds from all over the world, I gleaned some incredible insights about life—mine and so many others'. They never knew their teacher was, in fact, one of them, lost, broken, and desperately in need of healing her own life. This was more than a job. This was a gift that even now I would embrace again, if given the opportunity, and I would not even need to be paid. The Universe moves in mysterious ways, and we can never predict how and when the tide will turn, as long as we continue to show up.

Throughout the remaining chapters in this section, Empowerment in Baby Steps, I devote significant time to the need to know how much we do not control, trust in the "unknown" and find our power amidst the fear. Although we can read about all this and it will supplement the practical steps like seeking counselling or other support, nothing will be as effective as personally experiencing these life lessons. Once your dream to value yourself and be happy catches hold, some unknown Force will enable you to surpass everything that once held you back and you will be able to make that commitment to yourself to move forward.

One of the daily inspirational readings from Melody Beattie's *Journey to the Heart* says, "Learn to tell when it's time to search for another dream. But also learn to tell when it's time to move forward, through obstacles if need be, because the dream is electric, charged by Divine energy and love."[25] Pursuing a new dream could feel sudden, but it may have been years in the making. However, beautiful empowering messages like this one also often leave out an important part: moving forward requires that we prepare for and expect setbacks and self-doubt. My next story shares

---

25 Melody Beattie, *Journey to the Heart*, by Melody Beattie, April 1, Learn to Clear Your Path, 96
Published by Harper Collins 1996

how going from broken to breakthrough is not a linear path. The next step of my journey was about to take me through the holidays that had always been so special as a family.

I had only been living on my own six months, and then came Thanksgiving and then Christmas. I remember sitting with one of my daughters and saying quietly and sadly, "Families are meant to be together at Christmas." She wisely and gently replied, "I can't help you with that." It must have been so difficult for her to hear me verbalize my heartache. My wonderful four adult children had been so amazing and supportive to both their parents throughout the entire painful transition, and of course she couldn't help me; this was my journey, not hers.

The lonely struggle to meet my truth head-on and live out the reality of my actions was often overwhelming. I thought about my sister's response to my question, "How will I get there?" She sure was right when she said, "With a lot of pain." I knew that going back, rethinking and self-doubting my difficult decision was normal but counterproductive.

The breakthrough moment for me was to process that it would be up to me to create new family Christmas traditions that could be special and full of love, joy, peace, and promise. I had spent my children's entire lives showing them that this was the message of Christmas. However, this was our first Christmas with my new reality: I am divorced. I had to accept that there was too much pain and the wounds of separation were too raw to share a Christmas dinner with everyone together. I told my heart that time would heal many things, it would get better, and we all had enough love to get past this first one. A few years later, we were able to share more of Christmas together. But in this moment, I had to dig deep to get past the thoughts in my head like, "Whatever was I thinking of, leaving?" It was especially difficult since my husband was still in our family home with the Christmas tree, adorned with all the Christmas decorations that I had carefully chosen, often on our family holidays. I had left the special family tree intact on purpose; it didn't feel right to divide the ornaments and they filled the tree perfectly.

On a lighter note, I was too fragile to think of buying myself a Christmas tree that first year, so I bought a wonderful *Snow White and the Seven Dwarfs* lamp that still sits in my living room today. Perhaps it represented the magical way we learn to believe in happy endings from fairy tales; it healed a small spot in my broken heart.

Christmas Day came and went and we all survived. I shared a magnificent opening of Christmas presents and a decadent breakfast with my four children, as well as a great walk around Stanley Park. Then, although I had a number of invitations to Christmas dinner from caring friends and family, I decided to have a peanut butter sandwich with shortbread cookies for supper while I watched a sappy Christmas movie on my TV with myself. It was surprisingly OK!

Letting go of one's familiar past takes time and eventually brings growth, reality and a peaceful acceptance. One day a few years later I had a significant aha moment when I arrived home from working with my clients, who were all in various stages of turmoil and sadness. Right before my eyes, as I drove into my garage, there was another tangible example of "broken to breakthrough." The entire home across the street was gone, I mean completely gone. It was as if it had never been there for the previous four years that I had looked out and seen the residents come and go every day. It had always looked very poorly cared for, but it was somebody's home full of memories over many years. Yet with the home now gone, the vast horizon I could now see was breathtaking. I took this experience back to my career program and turned it into an entire workshop on transformation to renewal. I was able to personally relate to this as the beauty in the landscape of my life had already surpassed what I could have imagined!

This dramatic visual of the beautiful landscape appearing so quickly after the removal of the entire home touched me. It became a metaphor for me. I could now imagine that the feeling of a loss of self, however real, was not final. It opened my mind to the magic of what could be after what was. This showed me the wide-open lens one can experience once they actually take the steps to start over and entirely recreate the landscape of their life. None of the participants in my four-week career program could know that I too had recently needed to completely start my life over. This analogy was something my soul had never expected to have to face, let alone be able to share with others in similar journeys. In the depths of despair, one cannot picture how beautiful life can still become. Upon reflection I know that in that moment, I was still a very long way from owning who I was becoming.

Many of Anne Murray's songs continue to be a great comfort to me. A special one released in the midst of all my heartache was "On the Other Side," which I feel perfectly describes the journey of transformation, empowerment, and renewal in a beautiful way. Music is known to be a great source of healing, and it can enable us to take baby steps toward feelings of peace and empowerment. It is often the combination of the lyrics and the melody that can have a profound impact on our overall state of being. Do you have any powerful songs that help teach you lessons or offer comfort on the journey to healing?

A final story related to moving from broken to breakthrough happened when I began to offer a monthly workshop on managing change and loss. I read the poem "Autobiography in Five Short Chapters" by Portia Nelson at the start of the workshop. Many of the participants, including me, were in various stages of being broken to breaking through to a new level of acceptance and empowerment, and it could not have been more perfect for us all.

My understanding of its origin is that Portia Nelson was attending a class and the assignment was to write, in a very short period of time, how they would tell their life story in five brief chapters. The power of the message is found in the simple and yet accurate description of the five chapters of life: In the first chapter, the writer absolves themselves of all blame for any actions or outcomes in their life. In the second chapter, they are now aware of their responsibility, but pretend to miss the lesson and continue to deny any role in fixing their own life. By the third chapter, the individual attributes their behaviors to habit, acknowledges they need to make a change, and takes a first step. The fourth chapter brings the author to a positive action that links to the possibility that they can make changes, however minute. Finally, there is a "broken to breakthrough" moment when the writer makes a definitive change to empowerment and renewal by recognizing that at any time we each can make a choice, change our direction, and start a new life.[26]

---

26 Portia Nelson, "Autobiography in Five Short Chapters," in *There's a Hole in My Sidewalk* (New York: Atria Books, 2012), xi–xii.

Portia Nelson is a deep and gifted writer and I encourage you to seek out a copy of this poem in her book *There's a Hole in my Sidewalk* and allow its wisdom and simplicity to impact your journey of self-discovery on the road to own who you are becoming.

"Autobiography in Five Short Chapters" is both sobering and empowering. It makes the road to a new life out to be a very short one, and it also removes our excuses for holding any thoughts of giving up. At the same time, it paves the way for us to believe in our power to change. It demands that we take responsibility for our life and where we are and gives us the simple solution to begin anew. It is a process that may be repeated many times throughout one's lifetime.

The profound effect on everyone in each new group when I slowly read this poem out loud to start the workshop on "Managing Change" was remarkable. It instilled in me that we are not alone; we all share the same journey even though the details are different. We are all moving through various stages of being broken to having a breakthrough.

Any significant change is a process, and one often needs to take many baby steps over the years to really completely start over. When I finally left my marriage, it took many more years to be comfortable ticking the box "divorced" from the choices of single, married, widowed, or divorced. Everything within me struggled with this new identity. It took a long time to come to believe that it didn't erase the incredible family we built together and the wonderful family memories we shared throughout all those years. It was just a label, and it in no way defined who I was on the road to becoming.

There are many circumstances in which we might find ourselves feeling broken and like we need to start over, from becoming unemployed to an unexpected medical diagnosis or disability. These circumstances do not define a person's core being or limit their potential for great things. Yet, we ourselves sometimes allow it to do so. This, I believe, is the ongoing challenge. We must let go of thinking "this isn't the life I imagined for myself," move on, and trust that either there will be firm ground to stand on or we will be taught how to fly. Discover what could happen if you try, like I did in my next chapter.

Insights to Owning Who You Are Becoming – Committing to Showing Up

Second guessing our decisions and the absence of a support system can limit our progress. They can prevent us from staying the course and benefitting from how far we have come already in our quest to overcome our circumstances. Progress comes from both looking back and looking forward and noting what we have already achieved. How did you relate your life journey to *Autobiography in Five Short Chapters*? Can you write about this in your own words for yourself? What might be five different ways you have showed up as you strive to own who you are becoming?

Sometimes we can find inspiration and courage by reading or hearing about the courageous ways other people have faced life's challenges. However, it is important to never compare or diminish the magnitude of our feelings; they are real and significant for us. For me, reading beautiful messages from gifted authors every day has served to enable me to trust in a bigger picture beyond what my heart can believe is possible today. I now understand that these people were all writing from an original point of deep pain and feelings of loss that ultimately led to hopes for the future. How can you do the same? Can you think of a metaphor in life, like the home that was removed, to give a positive spin on huge change? Is there a poem or a song that you can draw on often to heal the various stages of your long path of changes? If not, perhaps make it your mission to find one that speaks to you personally.

Think of ways you have already taken steps to show up when you would have preferred to pull up the covers and stay in bed. Try to remember a time when you were especially rewarded for trusting, a time when you took steps to move forward and life surprised you in the best possible way. Build an arsenal of those stories to sustain you when it feels impossible to believe life will get better. I developed a personal mantra that I often referred back to during times of uncertainty: I would say to myself, "It will be like my first Christmas dinner on my own, it will be surprisingly OK." These are great baby steps to moving from broken toward a new beginning. What are some that might work well for you?

Chapter 8

What Could Happen If You Try?

The moment one definitely commits oneself, then Providence moves, too.
All sorts of things occur to help one that would never
have otherwise occurred . . .
unforeseen incidents and meetings and material assistance,
which no [one] could have dreamt would have come their way.

—W. H. Murray (1913-1996), *The Scottish Himalayan Expedition*
Scottish Mountaineer & Writer

IN THIS CHAPTER, I SHARE a few of my most cherished stories, stories describing my own experiences and those of others, of what can happen when we decide to change the status quo, commit to a goal, and somehow find a way to conspire with the Universe to achieve a seemingly impossible outcome. Just as it states in the quote above, "All sorts of things occur to help one that would never have otherwise occurred."

Sometimes things happen in our lives to shake our confidence when, through no fault of our own, everything falls apart. This can be especially true in the workplace. Many times lessons in the business world can be cruel and immediate with no apparent options for recovery. This can be due to changing demands for products and services combined with shifts in who controls the direction a company decides to take.

I've had such workplace experiences myself. I was worried about the results of a pending meeting with a supplier and I assumed I knew what was going to happen. I remember my brother-in-law saying once, "You are not there yet." He was speaking from years of experience and reminding me that I should not anxiously anticipate in advance that something will not go well. He was right. The outcome was very positive after all. That phrase, "You are not there yet," was one I continued to tell myself to manage my concerns whenever the stability of things appeared to be uncertain. And then, one day, you are "there."

Another story comes from a more significant upheaval at work. I had been part of an eight-year partnership in which I had initiated the lion's share of the profit-producing results, and I was the only woman in a team of four. I worked closely with one of the men in a subsidiary company on innovative and challenging projects using cutting-edge technology. We were a great team, and our talents totally complemented each other.

After almost two years of focusing on a major contract, which we were now very near to completing, the other two men in the parent company, who ultimately controlled this satellite one, decided to go in a different direction. They thought this new direction would bring more money into the company, and they were not prepared to wait any longer for the other contract to be completed. They had agreed to bring my partner into their operation, and there was nothing he could do to persuade them to include me. They called me in to say, "You can use your shared office as long as you like, but we have no job for you."

I don't remember what was more disappointing, that they knew my value and work ethic and still would not hire me or that they were willing to just drop this project we had worked on for two years and were so close to finalizing. The humiliation and impact of walking into that office every day, knowing that I was not enough in their eyes to penetrate the "boys' club" and have them give me a job, too, was significant. However, this became the biggest financial gift of my entire career.

No one ever knew, or even would have believed, the impact this conciliatory offer from my former partners had on my self-respect, but I took them up on their offer to use the shared office space. Since the phone line for the satellite company remained connected and was a different number from the parent company, I was able to continue the appearance of our company still being operational. No one would realize that it now consisted of one person, me!

I turned my focus to what it would take to close this $200,000.00 sale of an interactive educational CD-ROM to the provincial government. Since the other partners had lost faith in its viability, they walked away from the project altogether, including any potential revenue, should it close. Although it was completely a long shot that one woman could mobilize the resources needed to deliver the products and services required in the contract, I began the daunting task to see what could happen if I tried. Since there was nothing more they could take away and I had nothing more to lose, I was empowered to try. They had stirred within me a fight to prove to them that they were wrong. I decided that this contract was going to close and be successful if it was the last thing I did!

I already had the total support of the woman in charge of this decision with the Provincial Ministry of Education. She advised me to set up an appointment with the woman who led the counterpart division in the Federal Ministry of Education and ask, "What would have to happen to get their financial support and approval to proceed?" The woman replied, "A fifty-fifty partnership between the federal and provincial government." She gave her go ahead, and I already knew I had the other fifty percent support from the provincial government. Could it really be this easy?

We three made it happen! This is what can happen if you try. If you commit 100% to your goal and decide that failing is not an option, it is literally astounding how the "unforeseen incidents and meetings and material assistance" referenced in the quote at the beginning of the chapter will appear. You will get the assistance you need and could not even have dreamed possible to complete the project.

Two months after I had already started my wonderful new job as a career coach, I was advised that the contract for the educational CDs had been accepted. Now it would be necessary for me to call on every possible resource and person I could think of to be able to have this ready to deliver in six months while I continued to work full-time in another position.

My brother-in-law gave me $20,000.00 to keep afloat just long enough to see the project to fruition. My former partner, who was now hired by the parent company, committed to providing me with the technical backup to complete the contract. A close friend and my brother filled in the huge gaps of limited resources and lack of computer skills at the time to help me finalize the project.

Somehow, over two hundred and fifty CD-ROMs were ordered and delivered to high schools all over the province on schedule. Then, six months after that, teams of high school teachers participated in two state of the art videoconferencing events two months apart, with twenty high schools from all over the province attending each one. This was the forerunner to Zoom training, and at that time, anything could and would go amiss with the technology. This could result in the signal being blocked and the program being interrupted and/or terminated. I created the PowerPoint program and delivered the one-hour training each time, and a lot of the content I had been developing in my career program was able to be incorporated into the hour. I had no idea such incredible synergy would be available to complete the necessary details when the project was first conceived almost three years prior to this event.

Can you imagine? The former business partners had so little belief in me and the project that they never even asked me why I was using their boardroom when each of the videoconferencing events was broadcast or peeked in to see what was happening. Such was their blatant lack of interest in anything I was doing and/or perhaps guilt for kicking me to the curb. They should have been proud because this amazing contract was thought by so many to be under their company name.

The multitude of incidents, people and material assistance, which often felt like miracles that evolved throughout the fourteen months after the contract was signed, goes beyond anything one could ever have imagined! I was able to pay back my brother-in-law the $20,000 with interest that he had advanced to me and compensate my ex-partner for his help with all the technical logistics to complete the contract. All the other outstanding financial obligations were paid, and it was a proud and liberating day when I walked out of that office for the last time! When they told me that they could not hire me but that I could continue to use the office I could not have known that the outcome would far surpass the benefits of working for them.

Closing the contract and successfully completing it was only part of the magical winning outcome following the pain of being rejected by these business partners. Needing to look for work led to me finding a position as a career coach for hundreds of people from all over the world. It was literally my dream job that I never even knew existed. It felt like my life's purpose and what I was born to do, second only to my being a mother. Their decision not to hire me had truly become the best worst thing that could have happened. The outcome reinforced my mantra "what could happen if I try" forever.

In the same eighteen-month period of my life when I had to part with so many material things from my marriage and had been discarded by my three former male partners, I learned that I still had me. I could rebuild a new life. However, make no mistake, there are no free rides on this lifelong journey. I suffered an acute attack of osteoarthritis requiring two cortisone shots to get back to a functioning knee whereby I could walk without the support of crutches. This was all while completing the many details in order to deliver this contract. It was a sobering reminder that when we push ourselves to the limit, there may be some negative factors. You will likely have to fight for what you want and what matters most to you. It may be very lonely, and you may often doubt yourself and your ability to see it through. The stress may even make you sick.

You will need to practice humility and seek help from all your safe allies: your sister, your brother, your brother-in-law, your best friend, and your inner warrior. You will also need to believe that you have a direct line to a Benevolent Energy supporting your belief that you will be able to mobilize all the resources you need to succeed. You simply need to take that first step and decide to try.

That is the story of how one woman closed and delivered a $200,000.00 contract to the federal and provincial governments, working from her bedroom after her day job, in a "state of the art" technology well beyond her level of expertise. Although not everyone would have been able to source the advance funding necessary to carry the project to the finish line, it can be surprising what resources can appear and what can happen if we try. There is no way you could convince her that this was achieved without the help of an invisible Benevolent Source. See what could be possible for you if you decide to try. Remember that the dream is just the catalyst that sparks the energy to begin. It is up to each of us to be bold and seek the magic that will realize our dream. "Whatever you can do, or dream you can, begin it, / Boldness has genius, power and magic in it."[27]

You won't know what you can achieve until a switch inside you says, "Enough! I must take back my power, I must do this, and I must make this as important and consistent a part of my day as brushing my teeth!" It simply must be that kind of focus every day until you achieve your goal. Here is another wonderful example of how one person said "enough" and took back his power. I learned so much from watching on the sidelines when my amazing brother committed to losing 100 pounds to celebrate the turn of the century. Just prior to ringing in the twenty-first century, he achieved his goal and then trained and ran a marathon, never having participated in any significant sporting event in his entire life. He is for sure one of my all-time heroes and one of my best stories about what can happen if you try!

It is worthwhile to note that my brother first sought professional opinions to explore what could be done to help him feel better physically and emotionally. Then he spotted an advertisement about WeightWatchers®, and deep inside him, he found his own power to take the journey back to good health with a whole new lifestyle and community of support. He totally embraced the line in the quote opening the chapter: "The moment one definitely commits oneself, then Providence moves, too."

One of the most amazing stories in the music entertainment world that totally exemplifies the power of "what could happen if you try" is that of Susan Boyle. Read her story of how she finally decided to try out for *Britain's Got Talent* at the age of forty-seven and was initially almost laughed off the stage by the judges due to her age and appearance. She then went on to sell over twenty-five million records over the next twelve years. Well, she sure got the last laugh! Susan Boyle inspires remarkable courage to promise ourselves that we will never lose a dream by default simply because we did not try. From her very first song on the Britain's Got Talent stage, I Dreamed a Dream, to the beautiful song, Who I Was Born to Be, the first original song recorded by Susan Boyle appearing on

---

27 Johann Wolfgang von Goethe, *Faustus: A Dramatic Mystery*, translated by John Anster (London: Longman, Rees, Orme, Brown, Green, & Longman, 1835), 15.

her multi-platinum debut album, I was touched by her courage to move through so many obstacles, achieve her lifelong dream and share her God-given gift with the world.

Susan Boyle's story reminds us that sometimes we refrain from trying because we are influenced by other people's opinions, others who may view us with the same judgment that the judges viewed Susan Boyle. We allow ourselves to get caught up in what others think is possible for us. Know that such judgment is not an accurate gauge of our talent or worth. There are so many stories of individuals defying the odds and the naysayers. Embrace the mantra "what can happen if you try" and you will surprise yourself. It may lead to great accomplishments.

Susan Boyle's story reminds us that we can achieve our dreams before we know how and own who we are becoming before we arrive there. Just as Rainer Maria Rilke reminded us in the introduction of this book, first we need to "live the question." My questions to myself led me to write this book.

Let me share another little story that happened a few years ago when a determined mother found herself thinking "This can't be happening," even as it appeared that the facts could not be changed. My daughter had picked me up at the airport, and we were about to host an event with about three hundred people. We had a few errands to do, including getting some groceries for our room prior to checking into the hotel. My daughter was carefully carrying her agenda with her rather than leaving it in the car; it contained four thousand dollars to pay the contract workers in cash and, equally importantly, all the details and contacts needed for the three-day event. As she got back into the car after our last stop, she turned to me and said, "Do you have my agenda?"

My heart just about dropped out of my body. Instinctively, I knew that she had never given it to me to hold, even for a minute, and somehow it was gone. We retraced our steps to each retail outlet and turned the car upside down looking for it, but clearly we did not have it. As we slowly came to an acceptance of the facts, we returned to the hotel, checked in, and my daughter began making some necessary phone calls to her bank and other service providers based on personal information in the missing agenda. She told me to just go to bed and that there was no way we were ever going to see that agenda again. Throughout our working relationship, my daughter had shown me on many occasions that it was kind of fun to do the impossible; I thought maybe this could be another one of those times.

I was in an adjoining room, but I could not think of going to bed. I phoned the police and told them what had happened, and they said it would have to be reported online. I began to report the theft on my computer, and the online report told me to call if there was video surveillance where the crime occurred. As it turned out, the grocery store where we thought we might have left the agenda in our grocery cart did have video surveillance. In addition, we were parked close to the door, so the video would be clear. I called the police with this new information. The video showed that when we moved the groceries from the cart to the car, and left the agenda behind, someone had removed it from our grocery cart. Luckily the store manager recognized the person; they were related to one of their employees.

We don't know what happened overnight, but the next morning at eleven o'clock, we were contacted by the store manager, who reported to us that he had our agenda. All the money and EVERYTHING else was still intact in the agenda. We don't know what the police did to bring about this result, but it was certainly a miracle on the eve of our three-day event. This memory will forever feed my heart with the magic of believing something could be possible no matter how far-fetched that possibility might be. However, we always have to take the first step with complete confidence, as if we already know it will all be OK. Each successful outcome will guarantee to develop a new muscle in our capacity to embrace the mantra "what could happen if I try?" It is also likely that we will try new things more often.

In the excerpt below, I share further thoughts from the "Great Words of Our Time" journal written by my dad; these were original and collected quotes found in a special notebook and first referenced in chapter four. The quote below from my dad's journal reminds us again that we will need to be bold, and, that we will need faith in the process to achieve the magic, even if the "how to" is not clear:

> After our inner voice gives us direction, it will also provide the
> means for accomplishing whatever is necessary . . . In following one's

inner guidance, it is frequently necessary to make a commitment to a specific goal even when the means for achieving it are not immediately apparent.[28]

There are no guarantees for me or for you that we will succeed every time we try. We will not all begin on the same playing field with similar advantages; some will have more barriers to their goals than others. However, nothing can happen, under any circumstances, if we don't try. Go within and connect with the unstoppable mindset you have developed throughout your lifetime. It may feel like it is a bit rusty, but all you need to do is take the first step and begin to set everything in motion. Believe that karma will work along with you. Promise yourself you will not settle or yield to the naysayers, and then the impossible may become possible. The pieces start to come together when you are ready to trust that there is an Energy in the Universe that seeks to reward us and show us what can happen if we try. As we move forward with no compass, and even if we may feel abandoned by friends and family, we gain confidence with each step. When you try, you will surprise yourself, and your courage will find a way.

---

28 Gerald G. Jampolsky; *Love is Letting Go of Fear*, 3rd ed. (Berkeley: Celestial Arts, 2011), 32.

Insights to Own Who You Are Becoming –
Trusting in Happy Endings

People often talk about the "little voice on their shoulder," which is also referred to as our ego. It can sneak in amidst a moment of optimism and say, "Who do you think you are? This will never work." I was walking to my work one day in the midst of my divorce, and I sadly processed the idea that perhaps there are no happy endings; they only happen in fairy tales. Then I thought of a new saying: even if there cannot be a "happily ever after," we can still have the gift of living "happily every day." It was the beginning of my discovering the power of gratitude. This led me to realize that we cannot summon the necessary optimism to try everything if we don't first bring a childlike trust to each task. Have you lost that wonderful enthusiasm we see in the eyes of a child taking a first step, with no cares about falling down?

I didn't always believe in or even think about karma. However, as I began to reflect on many of my experiences over the years, I came to discover that the Universe really does have a perfect accounting system. Sometimes we are receiving and sometimes we are giving. You cannot know when a seemingly miraculous outcome will arrive on your doorstep. Sometimes you will have brought your blood, sweat and tears and feel it is "deserved," and other times it will feel like you just won a lotto ticket. What I know for sure is that so many things in my life could not have happened if I did not try and trust that some kind of happy ending was out there with my name on it. Is there something you could revisit now with a fresh outlook? Could you change your energy and just begin?

Think about a time when karma surprised you in a wonderful, unexpected way. Savor it, build on it, and let it shift your mindset to a level of optimism that can serve you and help you try more in the future. Remember the words of my brother-in-law—"You are not there yet"—and refrain from writing your own endings before they happen. What could you plan to try right now, with no guarantee that it will evolve the way you want it to? Start with a small project and believe it before you can see it.

The power to make something happen starts within us. We need to seek outside people and resources to help us, but always we are the final catalyst. Even music can be a catalyst—find a song that kickstarts your energy and makes you feel anything is possible. For me, it is the song and video for "Try Everything" by Shakira.[29] The energy of the melody and the delightful antics of the cartoon characters in the video are so fun. The message to try everything, even if you could fail and even if you make mistakes, because that is how we learn, is a powerful one to fill your head and heart with and jumpstart your day.

---

29 Shakira, "Try Everything," directed by Jared Bush, Byron Howard, and Rich Moore, 2016, music video.

Notes to Own Who You Are Becoming:

Chapter 9

Courage Finds a Way

No pessimist ever discovered the secrets of the stars,
or sailed to an unchartered land,
or opened a new heaven to the human spirit.

—Helen Keller (1880-1968), *Optimism: An Essay*
American Author & Disability Activist

ONE DAY AS I PORED through my treasured folder of special letters and keepsakes, most of them from my children, I took a walk down memory lane by reading a letter written over twenty years ago from my oldest daughter. The letter read, "I'm having a fabulous time! We spent the first day sorting out gear, then the next eight days in the mountains. It was fantastic! We are hiking and learning. We were rock climbing and crossing glaciers. I am learning so much about safe outdoor travel."

I would like to be able to take credit for even a small part of her love of the outdoors and her fearless approach to these daunting experiences, but I cannot, not one single bit. However, I got to observe, just a little, the amazing benefits when one embraces what they love and what feeds their spirit. The daughter I picked up at the bus depot after that incredible Outward Bound trip was definitely not the same one I dropped off some twelve days before. Her level of joy and excitement was unmistakable!

On the car ride home, and in an effort to connect to something seriously beyond the frame of reference of my city-living mind, I asked, "What was your favorite part of your Outward Bound experience?" Her answer literally took my breath away as I listened and internalized how terrified I would have been. My daughter replied, "The night we each had to find a spot to spend alone on the mountain with only some flares to send off if we were in trouble."

When you love yourself enough to dare to step outside your comfort level and seek to do what you love, even if it might be scary, you just might reach a level of self-love and self-power that you could not imagine happening any other way. My daughter had certainly taken that step when she committed to twelve days out in the wilderness with Outward Bound. For her, it was not about courage, it was about daring to embrace her passion of the outdoors. Courage to follow one's passion and be the type of person you long to be is one of the most important parts of empowerment and becoming; it is something I hope to illustrate in the stories I share in this chapter.

This same daughter was struggling a bit in believing she could achieve some of her lifelong goals. Despite her love of kayaking, she even asked me to take back a picture I had given to her of a woman kayaking down a turbulent river with an inspiring caption related to courage. She said since it clearly wasn't working for her, maybe I should hang it in the classroom for the career program; perhaps it would serve my clients better. Despite her doubts, however, she did have that courage—she doubled down and tried even harder and completed her outdoor guide training. So for ten months of the year she was a nurse, and every summer she lived her passion as an outdoor guide taking people on amazing trips in the beautiful lakes and mountains of British Columbia and in the Yukon. And it gets even better. My daughter then went on to meet her husband on the Chilkoot Trail in the Yukon; she was the lead guide and he was a participant. There is no other possible way they would have met as he lived in Ontario and she was three thousand miles away in British Columbia.

Courage opens doors beyond anything we might imagine. It reveals a depth in our character we could not find any other way and the possibilities can take our breath away. We plant seeds in each other's lives and we support and encourage each other to stretch beyond our comfort zones. It is a rhythm of life, and if we can be humble and open, it enables us all to rise to new heights in living. The power of courage can sometimes come from others and our desire to rise up to what they believe we can do or be. The next story is a vivid example of this courage.

This is a favorite story involving the same daughter, our family outdoor enthusiast; I shared it every single month in the career program during the workshop on self-esteem. Imagine it is early spring and you have been invited to go on a mother-daughter weekend to celebrate Mother's Day. It is your first Mother's Day living on your own in over thirty years. The promise of spring has a tall order to fill as it tries to heal your soul with its beauty. Nature is consistent in its seasons and it is predictable. Life on the other hand is not.

We set out for the famous Kettle Valley Trail with our bicycles on the back of the car. People came from all over to bike the miles of beauty at this magnificent tourist attraction. Our first stop was a bike ride through Othello's Tunnels near Hope. My daughter and wonderful guide on this adventure had, just a few years before, put her bike in a box and flown to New Zealand, where she biked solo three thousand miles across that country. At this time she was training to be an outdoor guide, so I was gifted with the best of the best while she practiced on me.

Biking through the tunnels in total darkness wouldn't be at the top of the list of places to bike within my comfort zone, but I was so thrilled to be on this adventure with my daughter that I told myself I would be fine. Little patches of snow still lined the bike path and my favorite butterflies danced across my handlebars. This was truly a little bit of heaven in the wonderfully safe and comfortable care of my personal guide, my daughter.

Then came the outdoor picnic lunch along the beautiful Myra Canyon— something I can refer to in hindsight as bribery. Lunch, can you believe it, was fresh shrimp and cream cheese on a croissant! The only picnic to top that was when I was in Ireland with my girlfriend fresh out of university. We were staying with my Irish relatives, and we discovered that in Ireland a picnic is a four-course event and even includes whipping cream. But after the picnic, the feeling of gratitude and the healing beauty of nature as we biked along the trail in single file with my daughter leading, suddenly ended abruptly.

I heard my daughter say, "Now, Mom, we need to cross this bridge. We get off and walk our bikes across in single file, and if someone comes from the other direction, we move over slightly. This is the only true trestle bridge with no side railings. In addition, all the others are built with no spaces between the trestles." Below, should you be crazy enough to look through the spaces on this original trestle bridge, was the magnificent canyon; the highest section of the Kettle Valley Trail was an elevation of over four thousand feet, so you can imagine my fear!

I can tell you that my daughter's words became totally drowned out and in slow motion in my head as they were completely overpowered by my thoughts: "No, no, no. This is not happening. What would ever possess her to think I could do something like this!?" My fear of heights was overwhelming, but I paused to ask myself, "Shelagh, do you really think you have come this far in life for it all to end on a trestle bridge in Myra Canyon? Where is that blind faith you have allowed to guide you throughout your whole life? Come on! Call up all you have got and follow your daughter's directions."

I don't think there was anyone else that could have persuaded me to do this. Mostly I didn't want to disappoint her. She said she would walk behind me. It was a long winding bridge with the canyon hundreds of feet below, and you could barely see the other side. I tried not to think about the fact that the only way to the end of this magnificent mother-daughter adventure would be to return and cross this same bridge once again.

About halfway across, two women were now walking towards us from the other side with their bikes, and from behind I heard my daughter remind me that we would just move slightly to one side. When we came parallel to them, she stopped to chat, as if we were all walking safely along in a beautiful park surrounded by green grass and level with the world, not suspended up in the clouds on a trestle bridge. I had to look straight ahead and see the end. If I looked to the side, the unbelievable height was too much, and if I looked down, except to watch my footing, the gaps between the trestles were too terrifying. I could not stop with her, even if that meant walking the rest of the way to the other side on my own.

I couldn't help but think this was payback time, perhaps for that first day of preschool when I cheerfully said, "This will be so much fun" as I was about to leave her, my firstborn, at the door of strangers with a bunch of children she didn't know. She must have been thinking, "What could be fun about leaving the safe peaceful playroom in my own home enjoying my own toys, sharing with no one, and having my own mom's freshly baked favorite treats?"

Ah, but the agony and the ecstasy of stretching beyond your comfort level! The power we give ourselves when we choose to feel the fear and do it anyway. There is a picture my daughter took of me on the way back on this same trestle bridge. I heard a scary noise behind me that sounded like wood cracking; it was the Velcro on her camera case, and I heard her say, "I don't suppose you would turn around for a picture." No, of course I could not! She was so comfortable on the bridge that she was taking pictures! I cherish this picture and all the memories it holds of that day. Only I could know the magnitude of what I got myself to do that day! This was literally a moment of empowerment in baby steps.

This is so much more than a fun story that I shared every month in the career program. It demonstrates that someone important to us can help us stretch beyond our comfort zone, but it is with our own personal inner strength when the perceived stakes are high enough that courage finds a way. And once you ride the big kahuna, whatever that is for you, you will be able to own it. We give away our power so easily, and often we forget some of our bravest moments throughout our life, many of which are only known to ourselves. Only we know when fear consumed us and only we remember what it took to "get to the other side." Only we remember when we felt helpless, vulnerable, and even faced with our own mortality. Only we know the fears we may still have to conquer. Only we know when we remained naked without a Plan B or a solution and had to pick ourselves up and try again.

There were so many courageous stories that clients in the career program shared during the workshops and we all benefited. I remember a young man in his early forties who was very shy and terrified of going to interviews and meeting new people. We were doing a workshop on goal setting, and as we went around the room, I asked if anyone wanted to share a goal they planned to achieve with the group. He volunteered and said that when he was fifty, he planned to jump out of an airplane. It was my nature to ask questions and I asked, "Why do you want to do that?" I just had to know the answer.

This wonderful young person knew exactly why. He replied, "Because all my life I have been afraid of so many things, and if I jump out of an airplane, I don't think I will ever be afraid again." Wow! He touched everyone. So many of us have a fear of social situations—imagine, he viewed jumping out of an airplane as less scary! Throughout the four weeks of the program, he challenged himself to conduct as many informational interviews as he could, and he personally initiated more interviews than anyone else in the group; I am sure he jumped out of a plane when he reached fifty.

Another story from my time as a career coach is a beautiful experience when a client shared a level of courage within her that surpassed anything I could ever have imagined. It was a life-changing encounter and a gift for which I will be eternally grateful.

A soft-spoken, vulnerable individual, with seriously exaggerated dark makeup and an overdone style of both her hair and her clothing, asked me if we could meet privately in my office. Each client did that at least once while we crafted their resume together. Often other personal issues that sometimes stretched my qualifications, as I was not a registered clinical psychologist, became part of our counselling session. In the latter case, I would typically direct them to resources for the appropriate professional help beyond my scope of service.

As I sat and listened to this amazing person sharing her story and what she was asking of me, for a brief moment my inner voice said, "This is beyond your frame of reference and expertise." She wanted me to advise her on what shades of make-up, what colors of clothing, and what hair styles would enable her to take her best self into interviews to ensure her success. This was a special woman asking another woman for advice. She was a transgender woman and was looking for extra support in an area that was new to her.

She shared that her life journey that brought her to this moment began when she was assigned male at birth and later worked in the highly male-dominant forestry industry in British Columbia. She was married and had several children. Not only had she gone through an entire gender-affirming surgery, but she also continued to live in the same family; her wife and children embraced her identity as a woman.

I had an overwhelming feeling of humility that she had placed her trust in me; all I needed to do as a professional career coach was help prepare her in any way I could for a successful interview. In that moment I became a student of life. This had become her normal, and she was asking me to make it normal for me too. Remember this was over twenty years ago. We discussed makeup, skin color, colors and textures of clothing, and hair color and styles. I was not a high-styled person, but I had participated in a class on the best colors for people, loved clothes and, with three very different daughters, had come to understand matching styles with personalities.

I don't remember her name, but let's refer to her as BC, for Brave Change. After our lengthy meeting, she was absent for a few days, and then it was the weekend. I feared that I had either offended or overwhelmed her. Then on Monday morning, BC came in as we were about to start and took her seat on the side at the front. When I recall that moment it still brings tears to my eyes. I was never so proud to be a human as I witnessed BC's transformation and the total acceptance and celebration of her by the entire class of about twenty men and women who had only known BC for a few weeks. The soft colors of beige, brown, and white with the classic warm style of clothing and her natural new hairdo style and appropriate shades of make-up and lipstick, so different from the harsh dark red she had previously worn, were all perfectly in sync with this gentle giant of a person. It was a stunning moment when the whole class saw her and collectively all clapped. They never knew about our meeting the week before; they just experienced this incredible "make-over extraordinaire."

BC gifted us all with a strong new frame of reference for our own expectations of ourselves; she had set a new benchmark of openness to the courage to change! She was such an inspiration and I am sure they were all thinking, "If she can, I can." Not all moments of courage require such a big leap of faith. However, each time we apply small amounts of courage we become more empowered.

Courage is relative and very personal, and what scares one person may delight another, as shown in the bike walk across the bridge. Go within and remember that you become more empowered with even your smallest acts of courage. These baby steps may lead you to be able to set the goal of jumping out of an airplane like the young man who feared interviews.

I encourage you to draw on your stories and others' so you will dare to do many things and trust that courage will find a way. Each time you do this you will move closer to becoming all you are meant to be. Courage grows with every baby step we take: "I am not afraid of tomorrow, for I have seen yesterday and I love today."[30]

---

30 William Allen White, "More Quotes by William Allen White, on His 70th Birthday," Forbes Quotes, *Forbes,* retrieved December 9, 2024, https://www.forbes.com/quotes/author/william-allen-white-on-his-70th-birthday/ .

Insights to Own Who You Are Becoming –
Feeling Your Power in the Fear

Can you remember a time when you were a child and you were fearless? Try to think of some things you dared to try when you were younger that you might not be open to do now? Can you recall how proud you were that you were able to, as Susan Jeffers puts it in the title of her book, *Feel the Fear and Do It Anyway*.[31] The only way past the fear is to go through it, and as a child we sometimes have more courage than is good for us. Then something happens. Our mind steps into the mix and many of us overthink things, hesitate, and we miss the chance to seize the moment. Is there something now that you could go back to and commit to feeling your power in the fear, just as I did when I crossed the trestle bridge?

Draw on something you have already done and forgotten about when courage found a way. Remind yourself that you do have all the courage you need. In fact, become your own cheerleader and create an arsenal of personal stories to feed your courage when you feel afraid. We need to dig deep, which is why I believe a daily journal can be a helpful tool to record some of our finest hours. A daily journal makes it possible to record the event and the emotions in the moment. One day in the future the challenge you are facing may be similar to something you overcame in the past and it will be a valuable memory to have recorded in detail in your journal. Then we can say to ourselves, "I know I can do this because I have already done something similar before. I know I have the power to be all I want to be; it is in me. I have earned my courage and can draw on it again."

I will always be able to remind myself that I found the power in the fear within me to cross that trestle bridge. Although I was mainly driven to do this for someone else, someone I loved and did not want to disappoint, I was the one who walked across and returned again at the end of the bike trip to do it a second time. I then later learned what real courage looked like from my client who fully committed to her true persona and being a woman.

---

31 Susan Jeffers, *Feel the Fear and Do It Anyway* (New York: Harvest, 2023).

Think of how you could try something now that feels scary but also feels exciting. We slowly learn as adults that the best way to get more courage is to go out there and earn it. Think of ways you could go and gather up some more courage; only you know what that might be. Remember that others may not even think the task you choose requires courage, so feel your power in your own fear, keep the details deep in your heart, and develop a brave spirit for each new challenge. Even as I write this story, I smile and I remember the fear I felt crossing the trestle bridge as if it was yesterday. I marvel that I was able to push through my fear and I am so very proud of myself. I encourage you to remember your proudest moments and draw on who you truly are inside and own who you are becoming.

Chapter 10

Angels Disguised as Strangers

I shall pass through this world but once. Any good therefore that I can do,
or any kindness that I can show to any fellow creature,
let me do it now. Let me not defer or neglect it for I shall not
pass this way again.

—Uncertain Source, Most Often Attributed to
Stephen Grellet (1773-1855)
Prominent French American Quaker Missionary

THINK OF THE WORLD AROUND us as a vast classroom in which people may cross our paths just once, or for a very brief time, and leave a permanent lesson in our hearts. In this chapter, I will share several examples of people who played significant roles in my journey of empowerment with baby steps. Each person changed the landscape in my perception of how little I control and how what I do not control may exceed my dreams and wishes.

Our friends and family can be wonderful angels in our lives, giving us words of encouragement and support when we need it. In this chapter, however, we are not talking about friends who are already in our life. We are focused more on angels disguised as strangers, ships that pass in the night,[32] guardian angels like those referred to in "Angels Among Us," a song I talked

---

32 Henry Wadsworth Longfellow, "The Theologian's Tale; Elizabeth," Poets.org, accessed December 9, 2024, https://poets.org/poem/theologians-tale-elizabeth.

about earlier in my journey. Although they may only play a brief part in our journey, it may nevertheless be significant and perhaps even life changing.

Now you may be saying, "Wait a minute, I don't believe in angels, so perhaps I will just skip this chapter." Please pause for a moment and think if there is anyone at any time that came into your life, even for a brief encounter, who made a significant difference. Perhaps as you look back you have always thought of it as just a timely coincidence. As I share some of the "angels disguised as strangers" in my life, I invite you to decide for yourself, were these people "heaven sent" by a Benevolent Energy in the Universe beyond our understanding, or were they all just a lucky coincidence? If you are open to possibilities, it may be that you have overlooked some of the "angels disguised as strangers" in your life.

Why does this even matter? I believe that this is part of the process that can contribute to your journey from transformation and empowerment to renewal. I have found that when we expect goodness in others, we somehow attract it. These may not always be strangers; they could be family or friends who surprise us with their timely appearance. These angels in our lives can also be teachers of important life lessons that we may never have learned any other way.

Do you remember my fellow Starbucks-loving hero from my car accident, the "angel" that I referred to in chapter five? She had just witnessed my car accident and was standing on the curb to see if she could help. First, another angel whom I never even met pulled me out of the car full of smoke after the two front seat air bags had exploded and I had passed out. I have no memory of him or his actions. He left me with this woman while we waited for the ambulance, fire truck, and police to arrive. Of course I was in shock but seemingly not otherwise hurt. Together we called my oldest daughter, but this "angel" did all the talking. She and my daughter arranged to meet at a Starbucks near her home, as I had declined the need to go to the hospital (which I do not recommend to others).

This became another story I shared each month in the career program. It was a story of kindness to foster optimism with my clients, a group of people rebuilding their lives who needed to become empowered to believe that life could be good again. However, what I didn't talk about was the profound impact she had on me personally when she—a total stranger—became the first person to whom I said that my life was kind of a mess because I was in the middle of a divorce.

I wanted her to understand why my being in a car accident would be especially hard on my daughter. I wondered what she would think of me. I did not anticipate her response. Well, it turned out that her very dear father, who was a minister and had been married about the same length of time as I had, was recently divorced too. She loved her mother and father both dearly and just wanted them to be happy. I believed that this was a handpicked angel for me who was not only a fellow Starbucks fan, but also shared a similar family story. What do you believe?

Although we lived very different lives and in different areas of the city, for over twenty years we continued to meet a few times a year for a latte and packed so much joy, love, and caring into a two-hour visit. Throughout the years at our coffee meetings, there were many indicators that this person had been heaven-sent to help me through those first few years on my own. This was a key person in my journey of empowerment with baby steps that I never even knew I needed. She was a safe and wise spiritual listener who cared with all her heart. She had a laugh that drew the whole coffee shop into our joyous times together. What a gift our friendship was! Sadly, she will never read my book, as she died very suddenly in November 2023. She was only sixty-nine years old.

Do you remember the woman in chapter eight, the key person in the provincial government who was strategic in helping me to close the large contract? She was a business contact turned angel, or perhaps vice versa, who appeared in my life on and off over the years. She never even knew that I was the whole company with whom they signed the contract. Six years later, a few days after I had surgery with thirty-three stitches in my face to remove a cancer, she texted me to say she was in the area and wanted to take me for dinner. I had not seen her for a long time. This was a very low moment in my life when I was struggling to get past feelings of "poor me" and revive my more typical optimism and my personal mantra of long ago, "Where there is life, there is hope."

She wasn't even a close friend, and it sure felt as if some power I could not understand had guided her to connect with me that day. It was just what the doctor ordered! We laughed and reminisced about the contract and other worldly things and then she was gone. She left me filled with the wonder and joy of life again. Perhaps in our times of great need for support from others, we are more sensitive to the gifts of unexpected friendship. These baby steps to healing and empowerment often come from unplanned sources to remind us that as long as we keep on showing up and trusting in life, we cannot know what will happen to rekindle our optimism.

There was also no way I could have known there would be an incredibly kind stranger, and for sure an "angel," waiting to make the transition to my first home on my own after my marriage ended as easy as possible. This move to a triplex was by far the most traumatic thing I had faced in many years. I had not thought about the magnitude of the adjustment of living alone after over thirty years with four children, a husband, a dog, five bedrooms, two family rooms, three bathrooms, and a park-like back yard.

A couple lived upstairs, and for the first six months or so I kept to myself. I was still totally adjusting to my new identity and still struggling with the new label that I was a divorced woman. We were pleasant and friendly when our paths crossed, but we knew nothing about each other. I preferred it that way. They would have seen my children come and go for dinner, and I was at work all week and often gone biking for the day on the weekend, so we rarely saw each other.

Often when we think we know how something is going to play out in our lives, especially at times when we have stopped trusting in happy endings, the Universe finds a way to create an ending we could not even have imagined. It might take an "angel" or two. Christmas was a month away now, and the sadness of this first Christmas, with memories of how my family always decorated our entire home together, weighed heavily on my heart. Luckily, there was a wonderful distraction; I was invited to my nephew's wedding in California at the end of November. At first, it looked as if I would not be able to travel, as this was the time of my acute osteoarthritis in my knee; however, the two cortisone shots made it possible. I was even able to surprise my sister and her husband in the airport.

This time together in California was magical. I could not know that it was about to be followed by another Christmas "miracle." It is a reminder that as we take baby steps on our road to empowerment, it is important to let life evolve and not anticipate sad events before they even happen; we need to build trust that something entirely different may take its place.

Now, as the taxi drove me from the airport and we came over the hill up to my home late at night, I was shocked to see it had been literally transformed into a gingerbread house with Christmas lights completely covering it, a two-story high building. The next day my neighbor knocked on my door. He wanted to ask me if it was OK that he had put the lights all over my balcony too.

OMG! I could hardly reply without tears, as it had been such an emotional unexpected turn of events. I had just gone from not even wanting to have a Christmas this year to loving the magic of the gingerbread house I was blessed to be living in now. I could have had many different neighbors, but I ended up with one who brought me exactly what I needed. What do you think of the incredible people that were living above me for that first Christmas on my own? "Angels" or simply good neighbors, or perhaps both?

The kindness and compassion of these neighbors continued. This same neighbor had a workshop in the garage across from my porch. One time he came to my door with a beautiful birdhouse, completely painted, for me to hang out in front of my balcony. Another time he had made a beautiful box out of incredible cherry wood that would win a prize in woodworking. Sometime later, I was very sad to learn that they were moving. Then, just before they moved, he arrived at my door to give me his stationary bike. This bike has served me well for years and probably is one of the reasons I still have not had a knee replacement.

Later I learned that this wonderful kind man, who helped to create the most beautiful transition for me to a dramatically different new life, had his own life challenges. He had taught me an important lesson in how to heal one's own life; it is to find ways to help others. This profound experience of kindness at this time in my life played a key role in teaching me to trust in the unknown and realize my future just might exceed anything I could even have thought possible.

I have come to call these people who have had an extraordinary impact on my life "angels disguised as strangers." You may think they are just people that happened to come into my life and coincidentally make a difference. However, I believe that life has the potential to be a magical, mysterious journey. If you choose to see it this way, it tends to build a trust that the right people will come into your life at the perfect time. It helps one be more receptive to saying "yes" to life and to also be more receptive to knowing how much is unknown.

It also reminds us that we too can be a difference maker in another's life. It fosters kindness whereby we can take an active role in creating goodness for others as well as receiving it. We can never know when something we do or say to someone else is going to literally change their whole day.

If we pay attention to our instincts, there are times when I believe we are divinely led to take action when there is no clear explanation. It makes it possible for us to become the "angel" in someone else's life. One day early in December, my first Christmas on my own, I found the most incredible *Anne of Green Gables* illustrated hardcover journal. It was released in January 1997, the very year my life began to totally unravel in pieces. As I held it in my hands looking through all the beautiful pictures and quotes from *Anne of Green Gables*, my thoughts travelled back to all the summers our family had spent in Prince Edward Island and the special memories of recently being there with my sister. I also thought of my dear friend whom I cherished and all the fun we had together all through our teen years. I only saw her once a year each summer when our families vacationed in PEI, but we remained very close, and I thought of her as one of my soulmates. She had red hair and reminded me a little of Anne of Green Gables.

We had kept in touch off and on throughout the years, but each of us were busy with our children and she lived far away on the east coast in the United States, so it had been many years since we had seen each other. I had also never sent her a Christmas gift before, but I felt compelled to buy this *Anne of Green Gables* journal for her and one for me too. I phoned her a few months later to let her know that I was no longer married. It was still hard for me to tell people. She in turn told me how amazing my first ever Christmas gift to her was and that she too had something difficult to share. It was as if I knew this was not an ordinary Christmas for her either.

One of her twin daughters, who, like her, had red hair and whom some used to call "Anne" because she reminded them of *Anne of Green Gables*, had been killed in a car accident travelling in a snow storm the previous winter. Years and miles apart, I felt overwhelmed with awe. I wondered what, or who, had guided me to send that one-time Christmas gift on her first holiday without one of her daughters! In that moment when I was compelled to reach out to her with love I could not have imagined how and why it was exactly the love and support she needed then. So, in addition to "angels" appearing in our own lives, we never know when we are going to be inspired to be one of these "angels" in someone else's life.

Not that long ago, as I sat in a wheelchair waiting to be taken on to a ferry, I noticed a young woman just ahead of me get up from her wheelchair and realized she only had one leg. One of the ferry workers asked if she wanted to be pushed down the ramp or if she would prefer to take herself. She was in her own wheelchair and appeared very adept at wheeling it. She said, "No, thank you, I am going to just let go and roar ahead of everyone. There is no need to tie up another one of your staff." I could not stay quiet. I said, "You are amazing!"

I could tell she would not want any sort of pity, so I did not ask any questions but she volunteered that she had lost her leg in a car accident when she was a teenager. She looked to be about forty, so she already had many years of practice getting around. Then, as I looked for her when we got off the ferry (they let anyone in a wheelchair go to the front to get off first), there she was again soaring full tilt ahead down the ramp. The ferry worker who was pushing my wheelchair to the elevator to the arrival floor thought it might be tight for the two wheelchairs. She dismissed that and insisted we could both fit. On the elevator ride, she shared how excited she was to be going to see her two children that she had not been with for a while. I thought, as she wheeled off, what a gift to have basked in such courage and gratitude. I imagined all the hurdles she must have overcome to go on to live her life with one leg. She was an inspirational angel to me in a fleeting moment. That wonderful woman was clear on who she was and what she had, and I believe she has been owning who she is becoming for a long time.

People that we never even know we needed come into our lives, and sadly, sometimes they go when their purpose in our life has ended. The number of examples of the angels who came strategically into my life at difficult times could be a book in and of itself. I didn't realize how much I would need them or wonder how I would find them, but they were always there. Slowly, over time, this all began to create a trust within me that everything would be OK even when it definitely was not. I found that the more often I took the time to journal events and outcomes, my gratitude grew, and so did my understanding of a meaningful life.

When I continued on the road as an observer of my own evolving love story, I became a happier person. This journey to own who we are becoming is a process that must be taken with baby steps. We have to take this journey by ourselves; it will take a long time and there will be pain and sadness along the way. We will need to pause and reflect often. However, it will be powerful and the rewards will be amazing.

My next chapter will build on these so-called coincidences, and you will discover that sometimes angels disguised as strangers collaborate and create the most beautiful outcomes. We must apply humility and know how much is unknown.

I would like to end this chapter with a powerful poem/proverb from a beautiful bookmark I have had for a very long time. This poem reminds me of how simple it can be to have a beautiful day and believe we are worthy of another one. It is an excerpt from the poem "Have You Earned Your Tomorrow?" It could be an angel's mission statement, or perhaps anyone's. Here it is:

Did you leave a trail of kindness, or a scar of discontent?
As you close your eyes in slumber do you think that God will say,
"You have earned one more tomorrow by the work you did today?"[33]

---

33 Edgar Guest, "Have You Earned Your Tomorrow?" YourDailyPoem.com, accessed December 9, 2024, https://www.yourdailypoem.com/listpoem.jsp?poem_id=3273. (This poem is in the public domain.)

Insights to Own Who You Are Becoming –
Knowing How Much Is Unknown

The longer I live, the more I am reminded that there is an opportunity to make a difference in every person's life that we encounter, and vice versa. We don't always find out what that is; often we are too busy or preoccupied. Sometimes we never even know when we have made a difference, like the brave lady in the wheelchair did for me. It is often in our times of great need that we are impacted the most by another's kindness. Sometimes we even think of them as angels and they enter our lives as strangers.

There will always be so much we don't know about each other, but, if we listen to our instincts and take action, we might light a candle in their darkness, as I did when I sent the *Anne of Green Gables* journal to my longtime childhood friend. Can you recall a time when you were forever changed by a brief and simple gesture or encounter? Was there a time when you were surprised by a stranger's story and it reminded you that we can never know what hardships another might be facing each day?

Trauma and grief in my life took me down paths of unchartered territory with no handbook on how to survive and thrive. As I grew to become comfortable with the unknown, I developed a more positive way of thinking. Throughout all the unknown scenarios, I was led to believe that amazing strangers would come into my life and I would be alright. The rewards for a simple gesture of kindness to us or by us can be huge! They can reinforce our belief in humanity and encourage us to take up the dance without always knowing how or why. Have you ever acted on a whim, or possibly your instinct, only to discover it was as if someone was guiding you to take that action? In the stillness of your thoughts try to let these ideas get your attention more often and respond. Listen to your heart and dare to send that *Anne of Green Gables* journal equivalent without knowing why. This can become a powerful piece in your journey to know how much is unknown and believe it will be OK before you know for sure that it is.

Think of the people that have crossed your path throughout the years. Write down in a journal what some of them have done that helped you to become more optimistic and consider how you can find ways to pay it forward. The more we can journal these wonderful encounters, the greater our gratitude for our life will be. These memories can plant seeds of hope to sustain us in the future. In living the questions that surround the unknown, we can each decide for ourselves: was this a lucky coincidence or a moment of grace? If it can happen once, it can happen again. Empowerment happens in baby steps and we need continuous reminders.

Part 3

Renewal
Will Surprise You

Renewal is not a destination that happens just once in our lives. It is subtle and can surprise us, sometimes after a very difficult time. It can often follow a time of deep discouragement when life felt hopeless. Then, one day, in the middle of all the chaos, we feel calm. Was it something someone said? Did we have a small win when we least expected it? Were we touched by a kind gesture from a stranger? The shift in our mindset to allow ourselves to always believe that something good is going to happen encourages our hearts to be open to life's surprises. The jewel in it all is self-love and subsequently the love of others. Renewal is an ongoing process whereby we are always becoming someone "new." Renewal is a daily, even hourly, commitment to ourselves. It requires gratitude, hope, humility, courage, and trust. Our stories, yours and mine, provide memorable insights to help us create a meaningful life. We can believe in a new dream. Our souls can lead us to new endings when we find our own answers. Renewal surprises us with the wisdom to rewrite our stories and own who we are becoming.

Chapter 11

Serendipity and Synchronicity

Serendipity can instruct us as much as sorrow.

— Sarah Ban Breathnach, *Simple Abundance:*
A Daybook of Comfort and Joy

FOR THOSE OF YOU WHO need hard facts and proof that some coincidences may not just be random events, you may find it interesting that some have explored serendipity from a rational and scientific perspective. In Christian Busch's book *The Serendipity Mindset: The Art and Science of Creating Good Luck,* he argues that there are identifiable approaches that we could use to foster the conditions to let serendipity grow.[34] There is another excellent perspective, *Meaningful Coincidences, Serendipity and Synchronicity* by Bernard Beitman M.D.[35] It discusses the two similar but different definitions of serendipity and synchronicity.

The stories in this chapter have been written to encourage the reader to reflect on events in their lives which, in hindsight, reveal meaningful coincidences that they may have previously overlooked; these coincidences

---

34 Christian Busch, *The Serendipity Mindset: The Art and Science of Creating Good Luck* (New York: Riverhead Books, 2020).

35 Bernard Beitman M.D., *Meaningful Coincidences, Serendipity and Synchronicity,* Psychology Today, https://www.psychologytoday.com/ca/blog/connecting-coincidence/202101/meaningful-coincidences-serendipity-and-synchronicity Posted January 18, 2021.

cannot be explained by cause and effect. As you have found out in the past ten chapters, I am all about the lessons found in our stories, and I invite you now to sit back and enjoy some of my best synchronistic stories that will challenge even the greatest skeptics. In my wonderful personal experiences, I have found that we are connected to a Benevolent Energy out there that cannot be explained, but I believe it is real. There is no doubt that sometimes the direction of life-altering events are changed due to a series of circumstances that we ourselves did not plan. Once we let go of our need to be in control of everything, we open the door to unlimited possibilities in a magical world of renewal and becoming. We discover the power of trust and allow ourselves to consider things that we never thought could be possible.

Either way, we are left with a curious sense that we should pay attention and that maybe we don't know everything we think we know. The following stories will offer some remarkable details that can only be attributed to an element of synchronization and serendipity; I had no part in creating the outcomes, other than being the benefactor of the positive results. The life lessons from the serendipity that I experienced firsthand, as referenced in the quote by Sarah Ban Breathnach above, taught me many of the ways that renewal will surprise us. Serendipity in my life made it possible for me to become more of who I wanted to be, someone who trusted life no matter what the challenge.

Let me start with a remarkable story that began in 2003 when I had now been living on my own for five years. I started to wonder how I could expand my career, and I spotted an article from the newspaper about "Management Training Disney Style." The combination of Disney and management training described in this newspaper article was such an exciting pairing for me, and at that time, I would have loved to be a trainer on management styles. But wait, it gets better. The color picture in the newspaper was from *Snow White and the Seven Dwarfs*! Of course it caught my eye, the lady with the nick name of Snow White for all those years who bought a Snow White lamp instead of a Christmas tree for her first Christmas alone. I took the time to cut out this article and save it just in case it became something I could investigate in the future. Then, twelve years later, this vision found a way to play out in my life and provide a substantial and timely income for me in a family business with one of my daughters. We became the first and only company in Canada to bring a three-day Disney management training program to thousands of people. They came from all across Canada, the United States, and even as far away as Brazil, and we were rated number one in the world.

In the midst of the period that we offered this Disney training I came across that copy of the colored newspaper article in my special papers; I had not thought about it for years. It instantly became something I could hardly wait to share in my pending book. Is it just possible that this vision never left me and deep inside ultimately played a role in manifesting it into my life? Now that is a beautiful thought, isn't it?

Another story involves a dramatic series of events that no one could have foreseen; it happened a number of years ago. A few days before I was to go visit my daughter and grandchildren, I suddenly became very tired. The night before I was to get on the plane, I lay awake in a lot of discomfort which I could not explain. When a determined grandmother is about to see her grandchildren, whom she only visits about twice a year, it is going to be hard for her to cancel her trip, so of course I did not.

As I got on the plane, I seemed to be rallying, so I was hopeful this pain would go away. The first night at my daughter's home, lying in bed, I was in so much agony, and the heating pad I had brought was doing nothing to relieve the pain. It seemed to be better in the daytime when I was up walking around. The next day I went to my daughter. I knew now that I had developed a fever, and there was a new red mark on the back of my neck, a bite of some kind; I told her I thought they were related. My daughter did not believe there was any chance of that; this was the daughter who was both a nurse and an outdoor enthusiast, so she should know.

After four trips to the local medical clinic in as many days, we received a diversity of opinions from "Maybe you have pulled a muscle" to "Perhaps it is shingles." Finally, by the fourth visit they were starting to take me seriously; after all, why would a visiting grandmother want to spend every day at a medical clinic? As luck would have it, I got the same doctor on the fourth day that had seen me on the first day. As she reviewed the notes on my file, all of a sudden she remembered she had seen something similar and knew what it was; poison from a tick bite was ravaging my body.

Serendipity invites us to be open to being surprised and letting go of trying to control outcomes. Each time we seek solutions and experience positive results, just as I did after four visits to the medical clinic, we are encouraged to be open to what is possible. The amazing coincidence of finding myself in another province and being diagnosed correctly, in just a few days, because the doctor had realized my symptoms were similar to another patient who had been bitten by a tick, is in itself a serendipitous moment. In addition, since I had not been hiking in the woods, the likelihood of any doctor in my province thinking that I had been bitten by a tick, in the heart of a city, would have been pretty much zero.

When I returned home, although I was now on the exact antibiotic prescribed for tick bites and starting to improve significantly each day, both my own doctor and another specialist were not willing to confirm it was a tick bite. Remember my reference to the challenges of scientists when confronted with a paradigm shift in chapter four? Well, this was another great example: I did not fit the norm for how one might get a tick bite. Having seen the horror stories in the documentary *The Quiet Epidemic*, which discusses tick bites and what happens when Lyme disease isn't properly treated,[36] I hate to imagine what would have happened to me and my life if I did not have a trip planned within three days of the bite and if I did not have the caring persistence of my daughter, which enabled me to keep going back to the clinic until they could make a diagnosis. There is no discernable causal connection between these events. However, after such a series of "coincidences," we are often inspired to consider the possibility of "divine intervention"; I know I was. I have found that every time something or someone grabs my attention in life like this, my trust in happy endings, that I had no hand in planning, deepens my ability to dream and imagine all the things I could become. Even when I face something alone, I don't feel as alone anymore.

My experience as a career coach also taught me a lot about the power of serendipity. Shortly after I began, someone came into my four-week program who changed my life forever, believe it or not because he did not

---

36 *The Quiet Epidemic*, directed by Lindsay Keys and Winslow Crane-Murdoch (2023; New York City, NY, First Run Features).

stay. He brought an interesting energy to the group in a fun, outspoken kind of way. He had some "out of the box" views on life and continuously presented everyone with ideas to stimulate their thinking and introduced us all to the phrase "There are no free lunches." It felt like there was a depth to him that I could not put my finger on, and I sensed there was a deeper story behind his lighthearted personality.

One day in the latter part of the second week, after he had come and gone as he pleased each day, he came up to me and said, "Could you take care of these until I come back for them?" He went on to say, "I think you might enjoy them." Among the books and audio tapes he gave me was the incredible book by Deepak Chopra, *The Seven Spiritual Laws of Success: A Practical Guide to the Fulfillment of Your Dreams.*[37] I had never heard of the author or the book at the time, but I highly recommend it if you have not yet read it.

What made this so significant in this moment is two-fold. First, many of the ideas he shared directly from the book became part of the career program every month. Secondly, the impact on me was indescribable. I was living in a temporary home about an hour's drive from my work for a month until I got settled in my own place after my divorce. An hour there and back to work every day was a lot of time alone to think when my thoughts were all so troubled. I decided to put one of the audio tapes in my car to distract me from thinking sad and worried thoughts amidst the huge changes happening in my life. In the audio tapes, the person reading the book was the author, Deepak Chopra. Have you ever heard him speak? He sounds like God himself; he has a soothing, deep, rich, peaceful voice, and you just never want him to stop speaking. Each chapter brought a new level of understanding about life, and the entire book gave me a fresh new template of thinking for starting my life over as a divorced woman.

The career program participant never came back after that day. Since I had no forwarding address, I had no way of returning the books and audio tapes. No one else in the group knew him. He had never included his email or his phone number in the application, so there was literally no way to

---

37 Chopra, *The Seven Spiritual Laws of Success*

reach him. I was never able to thank him for loaning me these inspiring tools which I then shared with every new group that attended the career program. Unfortunately, he never knew the amazing impact they had on my life and on all those who were in my classes—or did he?

Does it seem to you that he was simply the conduit bringing this amazing book and thought leader into my life at exactly the moment I needed it? Is it a coincidence that he gave me amazing tools from the messages in the book to inspire myself and then share them with hundreds of other people in the career program? Who or what had a hand in this serendipitous exchange, or is it all just a happenstance?

One last thought. On the inside cover of the book he gave me by Deepak Chopra, someone had hand written a quote. It was attributed to Goethe and I felt as if it had been written just for me. Here it is: "Our destiny often looks like a fruit-tree in winter. Who would think from its pitiable aspect that those rigid boughs, those rough twigs, could next spring again be green, bloom, and even bear fruit? Yet we hope it, we know it."[38] Is this not the best quote for someone who might be feeling that their life as they knew it was over and might never bear fruit again? I had never seen the process of a fig tree losing all its leaves after all the figs had ripened, in the late fall. Now I have and the following spring it's a magical rebirth. Nature gives new meaning to these quotes when you are able to experience the message for yourself; it is even more inspiring!

Serendipity can be dismissed or embraced; either way, it is profound and beyond our understanding, and it usually brings an energy of optimism. It also requires that we accept knowing how much is unknown, as we discussed in the previous chapter. I believe that as soon as we realize we are not in control of even the next hour, it can free us to focus on our role in becoming the best version of ourselves and embracing the path to renewal. We can stop rethinking the past, which we will never be able to change. We can let go of the uncertainty and fear that maybe some difficult

---

38 Johann Wolfgang von Goethe, *Wilhelm Meister's Travels*, in *Goethe's Works, Illustrated by the Best German Artists*, vol. 5 (Philadelphia: George Barrie, 1885), Book I, Chapter XII, https://oll.libertyfund.org/titles/ goethe-goethes-works-vol-5-w-meisters-travels-elective-affinities.

things from our past may be repeated. We are free to simply be and to become. I learned that by journaling some of the amazing, serendipitous moments in my life, I was able to release a believing heart that would allow itself to be surprised again and again, and, to feel more comfortable when things felt out of my control. It gave me the strength and hope to try more and free my mind from past fears.

In the quote at the beginning of this chapter by Sarah Ban Breathnach we are reminded that we can learn from synchronicity as well as from difficulties. Both happened to me after I had been living on my own for about six years. There was significant sorrow but what I remember most is the remarkable and "gentlest lessons" from amazing coincidences.

A biopsy had revealed that a very small and inconspicuous growth on my cheek needed to be removed. Over the years, after my malignant melanoma surgery, doctors had removed and tested a number of things like this on an arm, foot, or leg. They were all insignificant and only required a few stitches, and it was always done in the doctor's office. They were also all benign. This time, I was advised to go to the day surgery at the hospital, but still, no one had alerted me to what lay ahead. I was also not told the result of the biopsy by name (it was a lentigo maligna); all I knew was that it had to be removed.

I was told by the doctor's administrative assistant that I would be able to go to work the next day and would be given a local anesthetic, similar to the other times when little growths were removed. Still no one explained what was about to happen or that it would be very traumatic, especially since I was fully conscious. This plastic surgery required thirty-three stitches on my cheek, and a lot of manipulation of skin by the plastic surgeon, which you are totally aware of under a local anesthetic. I knew by the length of the surgery and the intensity of the procedure that something very dramatic had been done to my face. They covered the entire side of my face with bandages, and then somehow I walked out of this day surgery and drove myself home. I was in a total state of shock, wondering how this could have been allowed to happen without me knowing in advance what to expect. Why didn't anyone suggest it could be a good idea to have someone else drive me home? In addition, I certainly would not be able to go to work the next day.

On my first visit to the surgeon to have the stitches removed, I was ready to be completely transparent about my disappointment in how I was prepared for the surgery. The plastic surgeon shared some incredible facts and coincidences. I learned that the surgeon had reviewed the lab results a second time just before he did the procedure and he thought it best to do this extensive surgery. Why? His own mother had received the same diagnosis of a lentigo maligna. Therefore, combined with his medical training and personal firsthand experience with his mother, he made the professional decision to err on the cautious side. He was aware of my history of a previous malignant melanoma and wanted to make sure it was fully removed. When this mark on my face was first detected, it was not even the reason I had gone to the skin specialist; even this was an amazing part of the success story.

In the words of the oncologist who met with me after the plastic surgeon had removed the stitches, "This was close but clean," and therefore I would not require any further cancer prevention treatment. To this day, I don't know why they did not prepare me for this horrific surgery on my face. However, I also recognized that the seemingly coincidental fact that the surgeon had seen this already in his own mother, prompting him to err on the cautious side and perform a radical surgery, and that the dermatologist spotted it even without my pointing it out to her, is all amazing. Sometimes it can be a bumpy road to a happy outcome, and we learn to speak up and educate others when we deserve better, as I did regarding the preparation for the surgery. However, doesn't it seem that in the big picture Someone or Something had my back on this one?

I will share one last story from the plethora of blessings of coincidences that have happened over the years. It occurred on the day my youngest daughter was born. It was the Monday of the long weekend in August, and we were just relaxing in the back yard. My husband was about to start a new job, and the beautiful sunshine made it easy to just chill out, since I had started to be quite uncomfortable, with only three more weeks to my due date. No one was around in the neighborhood, and this was before cell phones and the benefit of being able to text people.

I made a routine trip to the washroom, one of many in a day given my pregnant condition, and started to hemorrhage badly. Our three- and five-year-old daughters were playing in the yard, and our fifteen-month-old baby was having an afternoon nap in his crib. My husband immediately called our family doctor, who fortunately was the doctor on call that weekend, and left a message. He then called my parents, who lived only about fifteen minutes away by car, but they did not answer either. He left a message that we were leaving the children to go to the hospital and asked them to come as soon as they got the message. And oh, did I mention we had a brand-new car? So, wrapped in towels and well aware after three "normal" births that this was a significant problem, we drove the ten minutes to the hospital in silence, each praying to ourselves that both me and the baby would somehow make it through this emergency.

In the next hour, what evolved was a well-scripted series of miracles, when one serendipitous event after another came together exactly when it was needed. My parents got the message within about ten minutes after we left our home and arrived quickly to look after the children. The family doctor phoned right after they got there, so my mom was able to tell him that judging from the alarming state of the bathroom, this was a significant emergency and that I was bleeding badly. When our family doctor reached the hospital, he rushed out of his car into the hospital parking lot and ran into the head of obstetrics, who was just leaving to go home. He said, "Could you come back into the hospital with me, I am pretty sure you are going to be needed based on what I know about my patient." Yes, he was right, I needed an emergency cesarean delivery.

Luckily, my doctor reported, just before I went under anesthetic, that both my heartbeat and the baby's were strong, so the delivery would very likely go well. It did indeed go very well, and I had the top obstetrician performing a completely unscheduled caesarean delivery on the Monday of the long weekend, when most doctors with seniority were off boating or golfing. There she was three weeks early, and my parents had a new grandchild within about an hour of them going to our home to rescue our other abandoned three children.

What do you think? Are these all just a series of wonderful and timely coincidences? Could there be a Benevolent Energy in all of our lives making sure it intervenes for the big life-threatening events? Of course we want to ask, why, then, isn't there always a happy ending? Why can't synchronicity always happen when we need it? There will always be questions without answers and there will also always be solutions that we did not create and can never take credit for happening. Who or what is responsible for these?

Who cares if what happened was a coincidence or truly a moment of synchronicity in the Universe? As the benefactor of these moments when the planets lined up, I know that some of these events may literally have saved my life. Other times, they shaped my mindset and I developed a trust in a "Power greater than myself," as they say in Alcoholics Anonymous. The facts are that every life has experiences they planned and others that just happened. I encourage you, as you read my stories, to look deeper into your own life events for wonderful new insights and possible synchronicities. This is a kind of energy that can greatly contribute to a happier and more productive life. It can help us shift our mindset from one of hopelessness to one with a renewed level of optimism. It can inspire us to find value in our life when previously it seemed there was none.

Every time we rewrite our story with gratitude, we strengthen our capacity to be more at peace. These personal experiences can play a significant role in how we grow to own who we are becoming. It is only when we pause to reflect on, and perhaps journal, highlights throughout our life, that we can take our gratitude to a deeper level. We can actually be in awe of some of the ways our life worked out, in spite of other ways when it was more difficult. This, in turn, deepens our appreciation for the gifts along the way and makes our optimism stronger, too. It did for me. Similarly, there is another gift in the Universe that can bring untold benefits to us, if we allow it; this is nature, and I will talk about it in the next chapter.

Insights to Own Who You Are Becoming –
Expecting to Be Surprised

On my road to own who I was becoming, there was a quality I had to develop; it was humility that made it possible for me to let go of thinking I had any control over my life. Of course, I could be responsible and prepare, but then I would need to hone my ability to adapt and expect to be surprised by events, people, and the timing and impact of both. It was often during those moments that I could not have scripted myself, like the head of obstetrics being in the parking lot, that I developed a confidence that surprise endings might be better than whatever I could have planned. Can you think of a similar experience in your life?

Serendipity and synchronicity can present us with life-changing experiences. I know I was meant to have the Deepak Chopra collection of tapes exactly when I received them. If I had known I would be rushed to the hospital to deliver my youngest child I would not even have been able to think of all the important things that all needed to be in place for the best possible outcome. I think it is easy to miss these moments. Think about how an event unraveled in a way that significantly changed the complete direction of your life. Identify events that you had no part in planning that became necessary to create a wonderful outcome. Are you remembering to be grateful for these and to make them count? It is so easy to allow these important memories to fade as if they are from some other lifetime and miss their significance. Recall them with gratitude and let them energize you now.

Unfortunately I have found that we are sometimes better at remembering times in our life when everything went wrong and ignore moments when everything went right. This can cause us to write our own endings and not stay open to how life can surprise us in the best possible ways. This is affected by a psychological concept of confirmation bias,[39] which is a tendency to notice or better remember information that supports our established beliefs. In our journey of transformation, many times we

---

39 Britannica, Written by Bettina J. Casad, J. E. Luebering, December 17, 2024, https://www.britannica.com/science/confirmation-bias

have a choice. We can focus on optimism and choose to remember and be empowered by the good things in people and our life or allow our established negative beliefs and memories of bad experiences to override this positivity. Life is a smorgasbord, but we can learn to shift our bias to optimism. It can begin with something as seemingly insignificant as someone leaving their motivational tapes behind.

You may be thinking this is not the life you imagined or wanted. Set a dream or goal in motion and take yourself out into the world and look for the serendipity that is waiting to help you achieve it. Show up, believe, and plan to be surprised. Know that it could take a long time, even years, like my "Management Training Disney Style" dream! Find a way to believe in your dreams and help make them happen.

Here is a final success story from pop culture to remind us about the power of serendipity and synchronicity. Julie Andrews' success began when she starred in *Mary Poppins* after losing the opportunity to star in the movie *My Fair Lady* to Audrey Hepburn. Even though she had already starred in that role in a successful two-year run on Broadway she was not chosen for the movie. Then Andrews won the Best Actress Oscar for *Mary Poppins* that year, beating Audrey Hepburn! Some describe these moments when things align to bring about the best possible outcomes by saying, "The planets lined up!" I call it serendipity and synchronicity.

Chapter 12

Nature Nurtures Hope
Without Reason

In the midst of winter, I found there was within me an invincible summer.

—Albert Camus (1913-1960), *Return to Tipasa*
French Philosopher, Author, Dramatist & Journalist,
1957 Nobel Prize Winner in Literature,
Second-Youngest Recipient in History

SOME TIME AFTER I HAD learned about Deepak Chopra, I discovered a beautiful book called *The Power of a Woman* by Janet Mills (we share the same maiden name, but no relation). It came into my life at a time when I was struggling to know what my strengths were. Janet Mills wrote this dedication in her book: "to Deepak Chopra, M. D. whose spirit and power have strengthened my own."[40] One of the quotes that Janet Mills shared that resonated with me the most was by Alice Walker: "I get energy from the earth itself. I feel that as long as the earth can make a spring every year, I can . . . . I won't give up until the earth gives up."[41]

---

40 Janet Mills, *The Power of a Woman: The Classic Wisdom Collection* (San Rafael, CA: New Word Library, 1994), dedication.

41 Alice Walker, *In Search of Our Mother's Gardens* (New York: Harvest, 1983), quoted in Janet Mills, *The Power of a Woman*, 49

As I attempted to move through my own dark "winter" and aspired to be a bud that could blossom again, more beautiful than ever, I embraced this metaphor from Alice Walker. It caused me to reflect on the example of how mysteriously and consistently, every year, bulbs, seeds, and perennial plants "hide" beneath the dark soil of winter. Seemingly nothing is going on to the naked eye. However, everything that is needed for the best possible next burst of the spring and summer beauty seen in flowers is happening without our knowledge of how and without our help.

Reality and nature remind us that there may also be the possibility for long, dark, seemingly barren months, perhaps years, and all the while there is important transformation going on, guiding us to the light. Just as we cannot see the changes under the dark soil in winter, we are not always able to feel the progress within us on our road back to a beautiful new life.

The closing of a chapter in our lives can come at any time, as a child, a teenager or an adult; it will happen more than once, and it always brings with it a choice. We get to make it our own story and assign whatever good, bad, and ugly connotations we like to the memories. Fortunately, even as we write the story and give it our personal perspective, we may, at any moment, rewrite the story many times as we heal. It is this transformative journey that empowers us to embrace the possibilities of a wonderful "spring" in our lives and find the courage to recreate ourselves and our lives in spite of what we had to leave behind.

I remember when we used to visit my parent's home my dad always wanted to show me some amazing flower he had just nurtured to perfection. I was always so busy with the children, and I wish now that I had praised him more at the time. However, the legacy of my father's love of flowers slowly found its way into my life and my heart and became a key healing element—but it was not until I lived on my own in a condo with a balcony facing south that nature taught me some wonderful life lessons right in my mini patio garden.

The first lesson I learned from nature was patience. My dad loved Easter lilies, and each year when he came for Easter dinner, he brought us one. I then read that I could put the lily in my garden outside and it would come back every year. So every Easter after the lily from my dad lost all its blooms, I planted it in our garden. It was so exciting to have our own

Easter lilies in the garden, and sometimes they grew again in September, not in April, and even after many winters, they all kept coming back. There was something very special about seeing Easter lilies in the early fall and realizing they were gifts from my dad at Easter time.

One year when I was living on my own, I wanted to try to do what I had done in my beautiful garden when I lived in the home I had with my husband and our children. My son had sent me a lily for Easter, and keeping up the tradition of replanting it outside, I decided to see how it would do out on my patio. Once the leaves started to turn brown, I cut back the lily and put it out on the balcony, hoping that perhaps it might survive our winter.

Now potted plants, as you may know, don't do as well as they would in a garden with all the lush soil around them all year. The following spring, I saw little shoots, but they were really kind of pathetic, and there was no main stalk and for sure no sign of flowers. I was going to throw it out, and then I found tiny little bulbs in the soil that had split off from the main one, and I decided to let it continue to limp along with its small green shoots. Gradually the shoots became tall, healthy stalks with beautiful leaves, and I was hopeful.

Slowly, as we moved into the month of June, a fairly strong main stalk with multiple shoots started to grow. Little by little, this struggling bud that most people would have thrown out became a magnificent Easter lily that could have won a prize. One week at a time, I watched each bud grow into a beautiful lily, and finally, there were seven giant Easter Lilies, all simultaneously in bloom. That had never happened with any of the Easter lilies my dad had given me that had been planted in an outdoor garden in my home. Not only had I learned the power of patience with a lily that exceeded my hopes, nature had shown me that sometimes there is no reason why some things blossom so well and others do not. Sometimes we can only hope without reasons and be patient and wait, as I did.

This was so much more to me than a "gardening success." This was a life lesson that I could forever look back on as a benchmark of what is possible with hope and patience. It was all the more special because it was connected to the memory of my dad and Easter. I sure hoped he was looking down because he would have been so thrilled to see me getting so much joy from my garden, and in particular from an Easter lily, a plant that he taught me to love.

The second lesson I would like to share came from owning a terrarium, now over forty years old. My dad gave me the terrarium at the beginning of my two years of cancer treatments. Even though I had continuously cut back the plants in the terrarium that were drooping or dying, it never did well in my family home because it got very little direct sunlight. However, it had a lot of sentimental value, so of course I brought it with me when I started living on my own following my divorce.

I could not believe what happened when I placed this terrarium in a window facing southwest with filtered sun almost all day. It thrived beyond anything I could have imagined. And then came the day to repot it using the same glass terrarium bowl but new soil. I remember setting it out on the lawn and having to actually break small pieces at a time to get it out of the glass bowl. This took a plant being root bound to a whole new level. There were about three times as many roots as there was soil, and I literally had to gently break the soil away from the roots so they could then be replanted with new soil.

I learned then that by putting the smaller shoots in water, many new roots would grow and I would then have multiple plants from the first one. I eventually made a "plant gift," with shoots from the original terrarium, gifted to me from my dad, for each of my children, as well as many friends and other family members. I was able to grow new roots in a glass of water on my kitchen counter in a matter of weeks. Dad never knew what a special legacy he left behind when he gave me the terrarium—or did he?

Now this over forty-year-old terrarium is so full of new growth that I had to buy a trestle to weave the many branches in and out of it. It literally reaches to the ceiling and it is in the same original large glass bowl. Over the years, I have decorated the trestle and the soil with butterflies, hummingbirds and rocks with the words "believe", "adventure", and "gratitude" painted on them. I can't even imagine how one could ever repot it as I cannot even lift it. My dad has now been gone over thirty years, and I like to think he knows how great the terrarium he gave me is today. It has become my "Jack and the Beanstalk" plant.

We can learn from this beautiful lesson in nature of how important daily light is and how it completely changed the successful life for the terrarium. Finding the light in our darkness sparks hope and fosters healing too. Just as nature offers no reasons behind its actions to us, we may gradually discover the power of faith amidst moments of despair. Another example of the power of light in nature is expressed in one of my all-time favorite quotes about faith and optimism from Rabindranath Tagore: "Faith is the bird that feels the light when the dawn is still dark."[42] Nature inspires us to seek our own sources of "light" to heal "while the dawn is still dark" and to find ways to believe a new day will dawn, in time. The ability to cultivate and pass on a "plant gift" to so many family and friends was also a way to use the simplicity of nature to "nurture" a legacy.

A third lesson nature taught me is how resilient a living thing can be when it is given the right nourishment and timely care, however small that might be. You can also see amazing results if you dare to cut things back when they have either become overgrown or died. Then let nature do what it does so well by bringing them back stronger and more beautiful than they were before. We resist changing things in our own life that have become overwhelming, and yet this is often the best thing we can do. Plants that are given the right amount of sunlight and sufficient water, even after neglect, rebound in the most extraordinary ways. Pansies can literally look dead, all drooped over, and within a few hours of watering, they are standing upright again in all their glory. Pay attention and give yourself timely care and watch how you can rebound too.

Nature reminds us that with the right "nutrition for our soul" we can regenerate our spirit back to its beauty. Just as some plants need shade and others require lots of sun, we all need different things to bloom. What can you consider cutting back and even out of your life that might be causing a part of you to wither, struggle, and perhaps even die a little inside? It is this natural order in nature of thriving with the right amount of light, water, and pruning that inspires me to know I have the same power within to care for myself, take action, and trust that I will find ways to rebound.

---

42 Rabindranath Tagore, *Fireflies* (New York: The MacMillan Company, 1928), 205, https://archive.org/details/dli.venugopal.844/page/n203/mode/2up .

Nature does not just offer lessons through plants. One day, in a moment of deep sadness when life, loved ones, and relationships felt especially fragile, I paused and sought a few moments of peace and comfort in nature on my patio. What I really needed was a hug, someone or something to breathe love and comfort into my soul, to reassure me that everything would be alright. As I sat there watching a white butterfly dart in and out of all the flowers on my patio, which I had seen it do many times before, something very magical happened. The butterfly came and rested on my knee for what felt like forever—perhaps a full two minutes.

Tears rolled down my face and I felt the power of love and the comfort of the hug I had just wished I could be given. Who could know this would come from the gentle presence of a white butterfly resting on my knee? Seek ways for nature to nurture the hope that you need for your soul; it can be powerful.

In my last wonderful nature story, I share my romance with the hummingbirds. It began when my son introduced me to a salvia flower, a wonderful perennial flowering plant that hummingbirds cannot resist. It attracted hummingbirds to my balcony for the first time in fifteen years. I had enjoyed a special summer because the hummingbirds came to visit every day, and often many times in one day. Then, sometime in October, they were gone.

In early December I bought a yuletide camelia plant with bright red flowers and a yellow center, hoping to attract any hummingbirds that might have decided to stay all winter, even though I had still not seen any hummingbirds for many weeks. I also bought the kind of hummingbird feeder you just stick into a plant on a small pole so I could be ready for spring when the hummingbirds returned. It was safely in the box in my home waiting for the first sign of a hummingbird.

Did you know that hummingbirds can return in the spring to the exact location of their previous feeders and flowers on the exact same day each year? They have incredible memories. One gray December morning before I had breakfast, I opened the door to my balcony, as I did routinely every morning. This was an early pause to start my day, a moment to breathe in fresh air, to appreciate the beauty of the color in all my winter pansies smiling "good morning" back to me, and to express gratitude for another day of health and mobility.

But wait. "What is that just about arm's length from my face?" I asked myself. "OMG! It is an incredible fluttering hummingbird. Where did it come from? I thought they had gone for the winter." Was this hummingbird trying to tell me that now was the right time to put out the feeder? Was it saying with its fluttering wings, "I am your Christmas present. I need you and you need me. Put that hummingbird feeder out today and I promise I will return tomorrow."

I decided to trust that there was indeed a bigger purpose to the early morning encounter with the hummingbird. I even wondered if it had been watching me open the balcony door each morning every day for weeks and finally felt brave enough to come by and ask for my love and help. So, that very afternoon, I carefully put together the hummingbird feeder, filled it with the special sugar/water solution, and inserted it into the special salvia hummingbird flower from my son.

I could hardly wait for morning. I remember smiling as I drifted off to sleep. Honestly, I just knew in my heart the hummingbird somehow had complete faith in me and would be back in the morning. I don't know why I was so confident, because I had not seen a hummingbird on my balcony for almost two months. Also, I had read that most breeds in Canada leave for the winter shortly after Thanksgiving in October. The next morning, just as I had believed, there was the hummingbird alternating between the hummingbird feeder and the flowering plant. It was a sight to behold! It was indeed an early Christmas present to me.

Bah humbug, you say! But this is an example of the joy that can happen for the believer who trusts, who lives by their mantras, just as I did: "what could happen if I try." I was so grateful to have decided to be prepared for spring in December and to have already bought the hummingbird feeder just in case it came early!

Over the winter months, I read all about the strengths of a hummingbird and marveled at how they could even survive one day. They became a symbol for me of the incredible wisdom of nature and how empowering it could be for us all if we embraced the gifts that we have been given and just went all out to use them for a full and beautiful life. Let nature help you find peace amidst the winter and thrive in the invincible summer within you. Allow the mysteries of nature to renew your soul.

Each living thing in nature seems to have its own perfect qualities that offer silent hope for its survival. We humans sometimes complicate things and allow our reasoning mind to impact our ability to hope when that might be all we have in the moment. However, nature nurtures without reason. Things in nature become what they are designed to be. What can we learn from nature so that we can become all we are intended to be? There is so much wisdom to be found in these little feathered friends, the hummingbirds, and what they are prepared to do with the unique gifts that nature has given to them for their own personal survival. We will look at some of the many faces of wisdom in the next chapter.

Insights to Own Who You Are Becoming –
Learning from Mother Nature

I didn't always make time for nature. I allowed my busy life to come first. Watching indoor plants surprise you when they rebloom and discovering how a little water can change everything are just small reminders of the many things we can learn from Mother Nature. Through the years, nature led me to the "invincible summer" within myself and helped me build an appreciation for how I too can transform into something beautiful amidst the difficult changes with the right nourishment and care. Do you have some special lessons from nature that you could apply now to your life to grow and thrive? How can you let more light into your life?

What have you already found in nature to fortify you in difficult times? Have you learned how effective it can be to prune back your life and cut out the parts that no longer serve you? I believe that one of the most wonderful things you can do for your personal stamina is to find activities that will take you out into nature. Having a balcony to watch plants grow is one of the most rewarding ways to garden. One of the most thrilling things I recently did for the first time was watch an amaryllis bulb in a pot inside my home thrive into a plant with seven beautiful blooms. For you, it could be gardening, walking, running, or even just sitting somewhere beautiful outside.

I have a friend who joined a bird watching group so she combines community with nature; this can be delightful to do alone too. On the West Coast, we are blessed to be able to sit by the ocean, but any body of water can offer serenity to a troubled heart. Find your peaceful spot in nature and plan to go there often. The renewal power of nature will continue to surprise you.

There is a world out there waiting for you to find ways to heal and thrive in it. What can you pencil into your day and your week right now? Don't let another minute go by without knowing what you will do to let nature nurture hope without reasons. Become aware of the marvelous mysteries we will never understand and thereby soak in the healing beauty in our world. We can become part of this magic. We just have to prioritize it!

Notes to Own Who You Are Becoming:

Chapter 13

Wisdom Is Not Limited to Age

The only real journey…would be to travel not towards new landscapes,
but with new eyes…

—Marcel Proust (1871-1922), *'La Prisonnière', the fifth volume of*
In Search of Lost Time, 'Remembrance of Things Past',
translated by Carol Clarke
French Novelist & Literary Critic

AS I BEGAN TO DREAM about the book I hoped to write, I thought of my grandchildren and all the things I have learned from them. It came to me that one does not need to grow old to have wisdom. This is something we can acquire every day by simply learning from all the people we meet and the experiences we have. These "life events" are necessary for wisdom to grow.

The stories in this chapter show how to find this kind of profound wisdom in a variety of ways and how it can come from many different sources. I believe that as we expand our perceptions of our lives and become more in touch with our soul, we gain new insights and wisdom about our life. In time, we are able to own all of who we are.

Wisdom can be found at any time of life. It is understandable that we often find it in our elders who have had so many more years of diverse life experiences. I recall my Great-aunt Minnie (her real name was Mary Anne, but we always called her "Minnie"), my mother's aunt. She was remarkable and lived to just past ninety. She had a quiet wisdom that just permeated a room.

I remember her coming to visit us when I was a teenager. We lived in Montreal and she lived clear across the country in Victoria. I had twin beds in my room, so she was my roommate while visiting. We had great chats, and she had such a delightful way of observing life. Looking back, I sometimes feel that her beautiful thoughts on love, loyalty, and duty have been lost in today's world. So many are influenced by social media and their time is often consumed with it. Once she said, "I see young people holding hands. I suppose a wee thrill passes through their hands."

She never married but instead looked after her mother until she passed away. She shared how she used to go on picnics in Beacon Hill Park in Victoria with her friend. His wife was in a long-term care home and did not even recognize him when he visited her. She shared how he was faithful to his wife and how grateful she was for his friendship. There was never any sense of sadness or regret about any part of her life. Her genuine gratitude for everything was a lesson in and of itself. Many will live a lifetime and never feel this kind of peace with life.

The way my great-aunt walked her talk and expected a lot from herself right up until she was ninety was an example of selfless giving and gratitude for simply being alive, and she always seemed full of joy. She would go once a week to the Red Cross and prepare first aid packages and other things for countries in need. She had a hilarious way of chiding herself and would state right out loud, "Mary Anne, what were you thinking of?" She had learned that it is in giving to others and keeping a sense of humor that we can find happiness. This kind of wisdom comes from the inside. We cannot learn it from others; we need to learn it from ourselves.

Little did I know that about twenty years later I would be able to share this delightful great-aunt with my four children. After we moved to Vancouver, she came to visit when my children were very young. It was then that I saw the incredible affinity that the very young have for the very old. They were absolutely fascinated with her, and she entertained them with her laughter and her fun games. Looking back, I can't help but think that we should find more ways to bring older people together with small children, as they have so much to give to each other. My memory of this beautiful person is one of respect and total admiration. It really felt as if she had captured the wisdom of how to be happy, which enabled her to enjoy everyone and everything with love and gratitude.

Wisdom is not limited to age. Therefore, when one slows down long enough to think about all of their life experiences and learns to own who they are becoming with each one, they will be on a steady path of increasing their personal wisdom. The more I came to realize that I would not be who I am without all the life experiences I have had, the more I became intentional on reflecting on the takeaways from each one. This is a type of personal renewal that can surprise us. We can think we understand something in our past, and then one day we realize that we have missed some big lessons. Time, compassion, and new life experiences often become the things that help us gain new insight into old memories and events in our past. Prepare to be surprised and be open, and you will grow in wisdom daily.

Just as wisdom is not limited to age, how we acquire our wisdom, and when, can vary greatly. Some Holocaust survivors have shared incredible stories filled with the wisdom that made it possible for them to survive. As I read some of their stories, I observed a characteristic that expands or limits one's individual capacity to gain wisdom from one's own personal experiences. If we intentionally choose to find meaning in our experiences, a way to give it value in our journey, this makes it possible for us to become wise well before we "age" in years. It is how I believe many of the survivors were able to live over fifty years after their desperate confinement.

Viktor E. Frankl committed to serving humanity and making a difference after spending three years in concentration camps. He lost his wife, parents, and brother there, and then lived to the age of ninety-two years. He was able to find meaning and his purpose from this horrific time and he shared this incredible wisdom by writing thirty books. One of his best-known quotes has left us all with an empowering message to overcome adversity: "Everything can be taken from a man but one thing: the last of the human freedoms—to choose one's attitude in any given set of circumstances, to choose one's own way."[43] He truly set the bar on owning who

---

43 Viktor E. Frankl, *Man's Search for Meaning*, https://www.goodreads.com/quotes/51356-everything-can-be-taken-from-a-man-but-one-thing

you are becoming as we move through transformation to empowerment and finally renewal.

My takeaway here with respect to the title of this chapter, "Wisdom is Not Limited to Age," is that wisdom "lessons" are available at any age. However, most importantly, wisdom is an inside job; it is strongly influenced by our soul's feelings about any given event, and it is also an ever-evolving perception. We hold the key to the amount of wisdom we can absorb every day. It can happen in an instant or it can take years. It is all part of our journey on the road to own who we are becoming. Wisdom lies in how we view all the things that have happened in our lives and it is key to our healing. The more meaning we can find, albeit in baby steps, the more successful our road to renewal will be; it is never optional, and its timing may often surprise us.

Sometimes the tragedies people have faced, and the stories in their autobiographies that they were finally able to tell the world, show a deep wisdom many of us will never personally experience. One can glean so much wisdom from reading *The Choice: Embrace the Possible* by Dr. Edith Eger,[44] another Holocaust survivor, who wrote her memoir at ninety years of age. She shares the importance of forgiveness, not only of others but of ourselves. She grew to own who she became and helped so many others with her work.

Eddie Jaku also survived the Holocaust and dedicated the rest of his life to promoting kindness, tolerance and resilience and died at the age of one hundred and one. He left the world with the legacy of his book, *The Happiest Man on Earth*. It was published when he turned one hundred, and he died the next year. Eddie made the vow to smile every day because he survived; he chose to focus on the miracle, not the journey.[45]

Each of these stories holds such profound wisdom about the power we have within to choose our thoughts so we can value life and overcome atrocities. It is a level of courage and forgiveness that is truly unimaginable.

---

44 Dr. Edith Eger, *The Choice: Embrace the Possible*, Published by Scribner, (September 5, 2017)

45 Eddie Jaku, *The Happiest Man on Earth*, (July 28, 2020) https://www.goodreads.com/book/show/53239311-the-happiest-man-on-earth

All these individuals shared how they discovered their healing power when they chose to let go of hate. These Holocaust survivors found a way to live such long lives with love and hope for the world and mankind. How can we too embrace this commitment to celebrate moments and chances, to make our own adventures, to celebrate ourselves? It seems that having the combined wisdom of hope and optimism and forgiveness contributes to a long life.

One of my "wisdom" heroes in the entertainment world is Dick Van Dyke. Although he has created laughter and inspired joy over eight decades, there is another side to this iconic comedian. He has been known to say that he never really felt like he was working because he loved what he did and has continued to be active beyond the age of ninety. However, he is also one of the first entertainment figures to go public about his alcoholism and I encourage you to listen to the YouTube video from the Dick Cavett Show called *Dick Van Dyke & Alcoholism: Breaking the Stigma on Alcoholism and Seeking Help.*[46]

In this episode of Cavett's show, Van Dyke discusses his experiences with alcoholism and recounts that in his mid-forties he sought help and checked into a hospital. Then he worked hard to reduce the stigma around the disease. As Dick Van Dyke grew to own all of who he was becoming, he used his fame as a comedian and found the humility to create another life purpose. He shared his journey as a recovering alcoholic to inspire others and make an important difference. Then he went on to have a life joyfully entertaining others and was also the humble recipient of a Kennedy Center award in 2021.

He has a remarkable life story, and I suspect his challenging struggle with alcoholism contributed a lot to his amazing desire to use his comedic talent to bring joy to all who were entertained by him. No doubt his ability to entertain others was in part because he had seen all sides of life and was able to understand his audience's pain points. Laughter is a special

---

46 *The Dick Cavett Show*, interview with Dick Van Dyke, created by Dick Cavett, aired November 14, 1974, on ABC, YouTube Video, posted November 17, 2023, by the Dick Cavett show, 20:28, https://www.youtube.com/watch?v=gcOlgyb_du4.

component of wisdom at any age, and he sure has taught us all what that gift feels like.

Elders have so much to teach us about the world, but they aren't the only ones. Very small children set such a wonderful standard for having the best day, every day. Imagine, as they learn to walk, they have no concern about how many times they fall. They simply get up, try again, fall again, and often even laugh as they go down and come up. It is a game to them. They commit to this process until they are walking like everyone around them. They act as if they have forever to get it right and that they will never run out of energy. They just go until they drop.

Children take living in the now to a magnificent level that we would all do well to mirror in our lives. For them, it is all about the moment. Could this be one of the secrets of wisdom? There is no self-judgment as young children try things; there is no failure, only try and then try again. They don't keep score or worry about how long it takes. Children remind us to have fun along the way too.

Now I would like to share some stories about young people in my life to show the power of youthful wisdom. This is a remarkable story about my grandson, when he was just three years and ten months old. Never had the miles felt so great from Vancouver (where I lived) to Calgary (where he and his family lived).

For fourteen days, my grandson and his younger sister, two years and eight months old, lay side by side fighting for their lives in a hospital room. No one on the medical team could figure out what the horrific bacteria was that was ravaging their little bodies. They called it a superbug, but no other child or adult in the whole province, let alone that city, had it too. It was soul destroying for their parents to have watched their two children at such a young age endure the pain of such an invasive lung infection; it required a tube to drain out the bacteria. They lived at the hospital, vigilant at their children's bedsides around the clock.

Mercifully, my two grandchildren were eventually strong enough to go home to continue to recover under the care of their mom, a former nurse in the intensive care unit. It would be several more weeks before my grandson was even strong enough to go down the stairs in their home to the playroom with assistance; at that point, it was at last safe for me to go there and see them.

As I walked in the front door, having been picked up at the airport by my daughter, my grandson heard the door, saw it was me, jumped off his daddy's lap, and wrapped me in a hug. That was the longest hug, one that I will cherish forever, and it was so emotional for all three adults to witness. None of us were prepared for his energy and joy at the sight of his grandmother. Somehow, I believe, in spite of his age and how seldom I was able to see him, he knew how much I loved him, how sick he had been and how grateful I was that he was better.

He then said that he would like to go downstairs with Grandma and tell her all about his hospital stay, which also surprised me and his parents. What transpired sitting on the floor in the family room was, again, something we three adults really could not have anticipated. I sat there in awe of his positive energy as he passionately shared all the details of everything he remembered from being in the hospital and his journey back to health from an almost-four-year-old's perspective. There was a wisdom in his storytelling that seemed to convey that he understood the magnitude of it all, and yet it was still in the words of a child who had just had an incredible challenge at such a young age and was excited to share how he won.

Now, all these years later, and following the many months of interrupted in-person schooling during COVID and long periods without in-person interaction with classmates, my grandchildren's wisdom, in a world so different from mine at that age, is amazing. I have become their student of life. This is another example of how, no matter what is happening in our lives and/or our world, we still get to choose how we will respond.

When it looked like they would be able to have the first in-person graduation in three years for my grandson's graduating class, I reached out to my grandson by text to make sure he knew I would be there. I asked him how he was doing. He replied, "I hope your life is leading you places you could never have imagined. So much is happening right now, but it's also incredibly exciting. I am living life and loving every moment." This is an outlook on life that enables him to find joy in every day.

At sixteen my granddaughter was already a voracious reader, so I sent her a sample from my book. Her reply was so beyond her years in wisdom and sensitivity. She wrote, "Thank you for being so open and honest about your life experiences. That is much rarer and much braver than it is thought to be. Thank you for reminding me to be brave and courageous when confronting the future. In your book, can you share when you had a difficult decision to make and how you were able to make it?"

Wow! We will all spend a lifetime on that question, won't we? It was amazing to me that my granddaughter had already identified two things that require courage. The first is to be able to dare to be authentic and transparent with our peers and risk their lack of approval. The second is to contemplate our future, starting with today, and make decisions based on insights within our soul but not founded on experience or any guarantee of a successful outcome. To even want to hone one's decision-making skills in order to plan for success shows remarkable wisdom at such a young age.

Another opportunity to learn more from my granddaughter came when we had an opportunity to spend quality one-on-one time with each other. She and her mom, my daughter, came to visit me just three months after I had sent her that short portion from my book. I had not seen her for nearly two years during the COVID lockdowns, and she had never stayed on her own with me. Her mom went off for a few days chaperoning her brother's soccer team in a province-wide tournament, so I was blessed with this wonderful house guest and the unexpected gift of time to learn the joys and heartaches of being a teenager in this era of the pandemic, with all the challenges of her personal world.

One night this amazing young lady, who could finish a book in a day, asked me if I would like to sit and read together. I could hardly concentrate on my book, as I wanted to freeze this moment in time forever. We had some amazing conversations, and in the card she wrote to me when she was leaving, she thanked me for being curious about her life. I was the one who gained so much from sharing a small portion of her young perspective.

Having a chance to glean nuggets from my granddaughter's spontaneous youthful observations led me to new insights about life. There is wisdom in realizing that it is the little moments in life that make life big. It felt like the many times together we had missed over the years while we lived miles apart melted away in those few short days. We can touch each other's lives in ways we sometimes cannot ever know, however brief the encounter, and sometimes it can last for a lifetime.

For me one of the most cherished pieces of wisdom I have gained is knowing deep in my heart that during difficult times, I will survive and emerge stronger. I know we will have wins and losses; we may get sick, have financial and career problems, lose loved ones, have broken relationships, and one day we will grow old. If we can build a "wisdom wall within our soul" and create a personal reference model to reflect on milestone moments, we can develop a frame of reference that enables us to trust in tomorrow. I have developed a mantra whenever something upsetting or disappointing happens in my life; I tell myself that "there will be a lesson," even though I may not know what it is in the moment. I remind myself that "this too shall pass." It helps me to trust in my future.

Wisdom can happen at any age, and we can observe a sense of wisdom in the very young and the very old and many ages in between; it is definitely not limited to age. Wisdom for me is to be at peace with our memories, to see value in everything in our lives, even the parts that have caused pain and the outcomes that we may never be able to understand. To be able to value all our memories is to be grateful for everything like my Aunt Minnie seemed to be, regardless of the things we missed in life and/or lost. Every memory is a stepping stone to something new. It is all part of our life, and it all makes up the total of who we are and how we are unique.

Wisdom, to me, is love, gratitude, humility, peace, and laughter. Wisdom is the Serenity Prayer, thought to have originated from Reinhold Niebuhr, that guides recovering alcoholics in Alcoholics Anonymous. This poem reminds us to start from where we are with a realistic approach, to keep in mind what is humanly possible, and to apply our wisdom to move forward. The version from AA runs as follows: "God grant me the serenity to accept the things I cannot change, the courage to change the things I can, and the wisdom to know the difference."[47]

Over the years I was always drawn to beautiful simple life messages tucked into stories to replace the fairy tales we learned throughout our

---

47 "The Serenity Prayer," Alcoholics Anonymous Great Britain, February 2024, https://www.alcoholics-anonymous.org.uk/magazines/the-serenity-prayer/ .

childhood. There is a special one called "The Wise Woman's Stone."[48] The story reveals what I believe is a core quality of the wise people in this world: the "precious stone" of life is not about the material things we have. Wisdom can be found deep within our soul; it is the peace we experience when we feel compassion for others and are able to let go of judging them and give generously. In the "The Wise Woman's Stone" we learn that "wisdom is not limited to age," it is in the wise eyes of the beholder. The man in the story returned the precious stone in the hopes that the old woman could give him what she carried within that enabled her to give away the stone in the first place.

There is a power within, like the one Mother Teresa also had, when we are so at peace with who we are and what we have that we can give to others with abandon, similar to the wise woman in this story. Once we move into the phase of renewal and discover that wisdom is all around us, in all the people we meet, we can begin to let go of many of the emotions that have held us back. This process is so complex that we can benefit significantly from learning about other people's perspectives on their lives. There is value in how people at every age experience their lives, and as we get older, we will quickly forget these stages. For these reasons, the young can become enlightened by the old and vice versa. Renewal is not a linear journey, so we would be wise to pay attention to the wisdom all around us every day.

And now, let's celebrate who we are. It is equally important to learn to give to ourselves. There is wisdom to be found when we work on growing the ability to love ourselves unconditionally, thereby making it possible to love others in the same way. This is what my next chapter will share with you.

---

48 "The Wise Woman's Stone," MotivateUs.com, accessed February 14, 2025, https:// motivateus.com/stories/wise-w.htm. Adapted from "A monk who was traveling," in *The Best of Bits & Pieces*, ed. Arthur F. Lenehan (New Jersey: The Economics Press, 1994), 73.

Insights to Own Who You Are Becoming – Finding Special Nuggets in Everyone

Wisdom comes to each of us, one step at a time, by living each day with awareness. A lifetime is not long enough to have all the experiences we need to make us as wise as we could be. In this chapter, my stories have covered the very old and the very young. Little children teach us simplicity and youth share their idealism about life, often with a deep perspective of the world as they see it. The older share their memories about what they have survived over a span of many decades.

Famous people who share their journey can plant seeds of wisdom in the world for a lifetime. But if we are open and take the time, we can find special nuggets in everyone and combine it with our own wisdom to rise to a greater understanding of life. Who are some of the people in your life who have inspired you with their quiet wisdom? Do you recall a fable like "The Wise Woman's Stone" that inspired you to think of wisdom in a new way? Have you made time to learn from the different ways people respond to life and tried not to judge them?

On the road to owning who you are becoming, wisdom is a timing issue. Some of the greatest lessons are often the ones that occur in our most difficult times. Personal experiences can be the most memorable. We read in the quote from Rainer Maria Rilke that first we need to "live the question," and then answers may slowly find their way into our souls. It can happen at any age.

Sometimes we are closed and unable to open our hearts to the "why" in life. Then one day "it" all just makes sense: why that relationship didn't work, how you healed in spite of the odds, what led you to a new life, and more.

Every age offers lessons to us if we are paying attention and willing to take the time to learn. We are often consumed with how we would like to change things and people. Sri Chinmoy reminds us of an important truth that can help us progress a lot faster. Let this wonderful thought guide your actions:

Yesterday I was clever.
That is why I wanted to change the world.

Today I am wise.

That is why I am changing myself.[49]

What steps could you take today to let wisdom grow in your life? Take some time to review events from your life and those of close friends and family. Can you find some special nuggets that you may have overlooked up until now? Step back and become an observer of your own life, as I have in many of my stories. Allow yourself to feel the wisdom that grew as you navigated through your journey of highs and lows. Planning to change oneself is definitely more likely to light one's way, and in the end, it is the only thing you can begin to control. Renewal brings us full circle from transformation through empowerment to the personal wisdom that allows us to see our lives in new ways and find peace.

Find some people in as many age brackets as you can and learn from them. Ask them if you can have an interview with them, write down some of the questions you have about their lives, and try to expand your view of life as you listen to their responses. Just as I have in this chapter, think about some wonderful things you have already learned from small children all the way up to the centenarian you might be lucky enough to know. Have your journal handy and take notes. If you are a centenarian, find a way to share all your wisdom with every age group you can, and go out and glean some new wisdom! There is always room for more.

---

49 Sri Chinmoy, *The Wings of Joy* (New York: Fireside, 1997), 118.

Chapter 14

Unconditional Love "Golden Retriever Style"

Do you know what you are? You are a marvel. You are unique.
In all of the world there is no other child exactly like you.

—Pablo Casals (1876-1973), *Joys and Sorrows: Reflections*,
Spanish Cellist, Composer & Conductor

IMAGINE IF YOU COULD REALLY embrace the above quote and start each day by saying "I am a marvel" (also defined as a miracle or a wonder). To me, a miracle suggests something that is "one of a kind," something to be cherished forever. This got me to thinking of how we typically describe ourselves. In the career program, we adopted a delightful phrase modeled after the book *I'm OK – You're OK*.[50] We changed this phrasing to "I am not OK and you are not OK and that is OK." This phrase suggests that we all have stuff to deal with and it just is what it is. We don't need anyone else to understand or approve of us. The goal is to embrace all of who we are.

The challenge, however, is that we ourselves cannot let go of two huge wedges between our mind and our heart: judgments and comparisons. These two things alone can preclude believing that we are in fact unique and realizing the miracle of our life. In fact, sometimes we even rewrite a

---

50 Thomas A. Harris, *I'm OK – You're OK* (New York: Harper & Row, 1967).

beautiful story to self-sabotage our lives and diminish our successes like no other might.

My passion to understand why we don't always love ourselves enough, or even at all, began with my dad. On different occasions I heard him blame himself for something that literally had nothing to do with him. I remember one day when he was talking about a time that one of his grandchildren had lost their way during their teens and he said, "How could they have done otherwise, given who their grandfather was?" I thought to myself at the time that this was as bizarre as blaming yourself for a plane crash just because you were a passenger. I also thought that the rest of the teenagers in the world should be so lucky to have a grandfather like him, and sadly, I wondered why he didn't think the same way and why so many of us struggle to love ourselves.

In my quest to understand all this, which feels like a universal phenomena, I turned to lessons in unconditional love "golden retriever style." It first began one day when I wanted to share a fun story that I thought most people could relate to for the self-esteem workshop in the career program. My children had grown up with the incredible experience of being able to visit a litter of about ten to twelve golden retriever puppies every year. My brother and sister-in-law were breeders, and they didn't give the puppies to the new owners until they were eight weeks old, so there was at least one delightful visit every year to play with them all. Imagine the squeals of delight from a dog pen full of twelve golden retriever puppies and four children all aged between six and twelve lying down on the grass with them! It was a sight to behold!

I used to joke with my brother that when he and his wife had a child, we would get a puppy. He would kid back that at least his "children" didn't need new shoes every year. A number of factors had prevented us from getting one of the puppies from their litters until this one year. It had been a difficult one for my children, whose classmate had lost their mother to cancer, a death that affected the whole school. My brother and sister-in-law had a litter of twelve puppies, ten male and two female. It was unusual to have such an unbalanced litter, and so the male puppies were not all sold in advance, and a few who had chosen a female didn't want a male. It was meant to be. We got one of those male puppies and called him "Lucky." He sure was lucky with all that love from my four children!

What I could not have known was the wonderful joyful journey I would have as the "mom" of this golden retriever. I wasn't the one who played with him, walked him, and spent hours lying on the rug roughhousing or patting him. However, I fed Lucky and whenever he was being disciplined by my husband, and if he was sick, he came to me. He always waited at the top of the stairs when everyone went down to the family room for the evening, patiently waiting for me to finish the dishes or laundry and come down too.

Golden retrievers are known to be herders and always want everyone together in one place. However, I just always felt the love in this act. He got silly and excited when we were all laughing, he stayed close to me when people seemed to be upset or angry, and he lay quietly with his eyes following the action in the room as if to determine if we were all OK. He was always there lying at the door until I came home from work, even when everyone else might already be home.

Lucky knew who the mother was, the "glue" of the family. This devoted behavior came to feel like a level of unconditional love that I never would have known had we not got Lucky. You see, I am not a "dog" person by nature, as a part of me has carried over a fear of dogs from childhood, having been bitten several times. Lucky always seemed to be in tune with my feelings, even when I wasn't paying a lot of attention to him. I thought, "If only we could do that for each other and for ourselves." There was no judgment when I had been too busy for a few days to spend time with him, no comparisons to who paid more attention to him; forgiveness, if I forgot to fill his water bowl, was instant, and he never kept score! Could we love ourselves that way? Could we love each other that way? How can we make love part of our nature, golden retriever style?

Years later I was gifted with another "love" experience with my son's golden retriever, Suede. The drama began when they came to visit and they were going to be staying overnight for the first time. My son wanted to make sure Suede knew his place when we went to bed. He was to sleep in the living room, situated between my bedroom and my guest room. My son closed his bedroom door, but mine was left open—I was in the habit of doing so since, living alone, there was typically never a reason for me to close my door. To make sure Suede remembered his place, my son put chairs in front of my open doorway.

Well, not too long after the door to my son's bedroom closed, Suede set about to moving the chairs, just enough so he could slip into my bedroom. When my son got up a little later to use the washroom, he discovered that Suede had disobeyed what he had specifically laid out as the acceptable sleeping arrangements. The next time he came, my son brought the dog gate, since Suede was usually intimidated by it. However, Suede even slid past the gate and found his way to lie beside my bed. Again, my son was clearly not impressed with his disobedience.

Very quickly we realized that it really wasn't a problem for Suede to sleep by my bed, and we stopped blocking the doorway, as it didn't work anyway. Suede came to know the routine and as soon as we went to brush our teeth he would go and lie by my bed as if to say, "This is my spot and I am claiming it." Did he want to protect me, a person that he sensed was very important to his master? He just lay by my bed all night. Even when I got up to use the ensuite washroom, he barely stirred until morning. If he did move at all, it was only to lay across the door opening so that I couldn't leave my bedroom without him knowing it. For me, this was another journey of understanding an amazing level of unconditional and unexplainable love.

The mystery and commitment of this caring and protective behavior will never really be solved as Suede, of course, could not talk. Also, he has now been gone for several years. I cherish the memory of my son's dog and his love that I can't even claim to have deserved. I didn't take him for great walks or look after him for more than a few hours when my son would work a day in my city. However, this special love and attention from Suede is something in my life journey that will touch me forever and for which I will be eternally grateful. We can learn a lot about "forever love" and unconditional love from our pets.

Golden retrievers always assume you are glad to see them and they put their entire body into greeting you with enthusiasm; they make loving look so spontaneous and incredibly easy. Doing this can actually be hard—especially if we are talking about loving ourselves. Self-love is an art. Self-love is complicated. Self-love is a journey, not a destination. It's not a place we reach and can say we're "there" forever. Painful thoughts are never completely erased because when we bury our feelings, they are still alive; some we know and recognize, others seem to come out of nowhere.

A golden retriever is focused on "herding" the family altogether and loving each member equally. It is easy to assume love is their dominant driver by observing their behavior; there are no comparisons and judgments of either you or them. They can misbehave in one moment and in the next win you over with their wonderful energy and enthusiasm. Now let's compare this to what we do. Our conscious thoughts, sometimes referred to as our ego, strive to control our thinking. Our subconscious thoughts, forming over eighty per-cent, almost all of which are negative, can often override our best interests. Think of a bridge with your conscious thoughts on one side of the bridge standing strong, bold and known. Then the subconscious thoughts are lurking hidden on the other side of the bridge and unknown. How can they work together to bring the best that each has to offer and create a beautiful result?

How can we ever hope to love ourselves unconditionally, even knowing all the imperfections, broken promises, missed opportunities, procrastinated goals, and ignored dreams? Add to this mix the stories we have told ourselves, some of which aren't even correct. Even a few steps toward the middle of the bridge may cause the glass bubble protecting one's heart, mind, and soul to crack. How can we strengthen our conscious thoughts enough to find meaning and purpose in all of who we are and understand that we can always choose to be in a state of becoming more of our best self? What will it take to let forgiveness lead the way to unconditional self-love?

Let's learn from the golden retriever. Anyone who has had a golden knows their capacity to misbehave. However, as I mentioned above, the time span between the naughty behavior and that endearing "let's just have a cuddle and love each other" is usually a nanosecond. On the other hand, we humans often need a long time to let go of things that happen. Meeting in the middle of the bridge, where we are able to nurture the mind, feed the soul with kindness, and set realistic expectations may be a lifelong project. Unconditionally loving yourself will be like excelling at playing a musical instrument; you will need to practice every day. You will never achieve perfection. My sister shared a phrase once with me that feels very comfortable when I think of loving myself unconditionally: "It doesn't have to be perfect to be perfect." The challenge with moving towards the best possible version of self-love is it needs consistency. It is so easy to slip backwards.

In the quiet moments alone with yourself and your thoughts, take time to write out a letter of encouragement to yourself that you can read daily. This is one that I crafted for myself:

I am not perfect. There are things I have left unsaid, dreams I have not fulfilled that I had the power to complete, people I have hurt intentionally and unintentionally, unrealistic goals I have set and then blamed myself for falling short of achieving, times when I could have tried harder and I walked away, people I have chosen not to understand or forgive and moments in life I wish I could do again and do better. There are words out there from me that can never be retrieved or erased, phone calls I never made or returned, and text messages I never answered. But through it all, I am human, and each day I try again to learn and grow and be better. Each day I reflect on how I have made a difference and will continue to, after I am gone. I show up and dare to try harder, to be kind and let go of all my judgments. I try not to compare myself to others, but sometimes it seems as if everyone else gets it right but me. I try to take the best and leave the rest. I accept that I am not OK and that is OK.

Every day is a gift, and every day, one day at a time, creates a whole life. However, some days are what my brother calls "lay low days." Days like this might be a good time to bring out the letter you wrote to yourself and take being kind to yourself to a new level of compassion. Can you apply the concept of unconditional love golden retriever style to loving yourself?

Therapy, along with support and encouragement from family and friends, can help us overcome deep feelings of despair with ourselves and our lives. These resources can help to remind us of the ways that we often don't have full control over our lives and the things that have happened. However, self-love is personal and unique—a one-of-a-kind process. You cannot do it alone and yet you must do it alone because you are the only one who can sign off on all your perceived debts to others and to yourself. You alone hold the keys to unconditionally loving all your life moments and valuing the contributions they have made to make you the magnificent human spirit you are today. Forgiving yourself is an inside job! Trust that life will unfold, your soul will continue to collaborate with a Power greater than yourself, and through it all, you will find a way to continue awakening to self-love. You will grow to embrace the message, "It doesn't have to be perfect to be perfect" and "I am not OK and that is OK."

There is a powerful emotion unknown to a golden retriever; it is apathy. Have you ever watched them enter a room full of people? Their entire body is consumed with enthusiasm and love as they rush to greet every single person. It feels as if this is the one emotion that separates us from the unconditional love of a golden retriever. They simply exude love and compassion, even with strangers. However, we can sometimes choose apathy as a way to protect ourselves, especially in times of self-doubt and low self-esteem. It can be what happens when past hurts go so deep that healing feels impossible.

We may be tempted to give up on ourselves and decide there is no hope of a reconciliation and no way we can think of loving ourselves again. However, I believe we humans are capable of extraordinary possibilities. We can open a new door to a new room called compassion in the otherwise empty home. This is where the real magic takes place. If we can take responsibility for the perceptions we need to manage within ourselves, we can become free in a beautiful new way. This relationship we are talking about is the one we have with ourselves; it could even be the one we have with our ego and our soul. Apathy can impact relationships with others, as well, and so it is something we need to process and address.

I learned a lot from getting to know more about the recovering alcoholics that my dad often invited for dinner. For many of them, to be able to love themselves enough to start over, they had to get past the deep disappointment they felt within themselves for the people they hurt along the way. It is always such a gift when grace intervenes and paves the way. Always, we need to remember we are only human.

So what about compassion for ourselves? I learned from one of the best, my dad, that there is a profound healing power in the ability to be able to laugh at our mistakes and view complex life questions with humor. I still love the cartoons from the *Dear God Kids* era whereby children presented God with delightful thoughts, sometimes addressing complicated issues.

The cartoons of the kids enhanced each response by infusing it with a wonderful visual of the simplicity and honesty of children. Here is one of my favorites: "Dear God, when you forgive do you use an eraser?"[51] Of course we do not, and worse still, we may embellish a mistake over time, sometimes our own and other times someone else's—instead of letting it go.

Self-love requires that we commit to being our own best friend. Have you ever noticed how easily a friend can encourage you and not themselves? They have chosen to love you as you are, not because you are perfect. They do not judge you and there is no gray line between loving you and accepting you. To them you are enough! Can you do the same for yourself?

Find a way to walk into your light. Often we resist, hold back, and think, "I am not worthy." You are worthy simply for showing up when it was hard, for being vulnerable when you wanted to hide, for trusting the unknown until it felt more familiar. These are all important steps we need to take on the road to owning who we are becoming.

Seek out your nuggets of joy and have a daily routine that fosters healing. Here are some of mine: The Serenity Prayer, gratitude, exercise, nature, music, laughter, community, nutrition, and a daily reading of something inspiring, a beautiful quote or affirmation. "Moments of joy" can be what keeps one able to manage the dark days. What does a moment of joy look like to you? Create a vision in your mind, or better still, take a picture of it, if you can; and place it where you will be able to see it often.

This is the fourth chapter in the section on how "Renewal Will Surprise You." We are getting close to the conclusion of our journey on the road to owning who you are becoming. You have already experienced that the steps to renewal in this section are not intended to be complex psychological steps. They are instead ideas that I found healed me after a lot of struggles with self-love and forgiveness. I discovered that paying attention to the serendipitous moments, the mysteries of nature, and the beauty of wisdom in all ages has guided me to value this precious gift of life. It is too short to

---

51 Annie Fitzgerald, September image, *Dear God Kids 1985 Calendar* (Allen, TX: Argus Communications, Intercontinental Greetings Ltd., 1984).

focus on where we could have done things differently. We only know we have this moment to build on and find out what makes our heart sing.

When I paused long enough to reflect on my journey, write this book and finally publish it at the age of eighty, it struck me that we must each strive to reflect on our lives. Part of self-love is taking time to cherish how you reached this moment and the greatness of the trip you have already had, in spite of the challenges. Begin to proudly own who you are becoming. My hope is that you will start today. Every single day needs to have a routine of joyful activities. Make time to lay out what yours will be. Seek professional help if you need to, as well as support groups and friends and family who relate to what you love, and have a program for daily renewal. Throughout my continuous quest to understand life a little better, especially when it disappoints me, I try to focus on the beautiful mysteries of life, and how I can achieve more gratitude, hope, humility, and trust.

Here is one last story from my days as a career coach that dramatically demonstrates how we can nourish or sabotage our ability to love ourselves. Anytime I am thinking about the power we have to be our best advocate or our greatest critic, I am reminded of this woman in one of the programs. It began when we were talking about the role we play in magnifying or diminishing our self-confidence. Suddenly a woman put up her hand and wanted to share the impact on her of a bad performance review. Much to my horror, although this had occurred several years ago and was, in her words, the only bad review she had ever received, she actually carried it with her in her purse every day! This takes self-sabotage to a whole new level.

Later, we had a conversation in my office, and she agreed to leave it with me overnight and to decide, by the next day, if she would actually destroy it. The next day when we met, she confessed that she still had a copy of this review and that was the only way she was able to leave one with me. Eventually she started to tear them both into multiple pieces; she behaved like a "human shredder" and I felt I was experiencing the power of letting go of one's baggage in a most extraordinary way. I also hoped there wasn't a third copy anywhere.

If we are truly honest with ourselves, this could be anyone's story, one in a different setting but with the same theme: holding onto the thoughts that we would be better to let go. Think about the negative things people have said to you that have impacted your ability to value and love yourself, perhaps years ago, that you still remember. Why? Hurtful words are difficult to erase from our hearts. What can we do to counter this known fact?

First, we can acknowledge the hurt. Then we can make a commitment to balance the scale with an arsenal of positivity. I suggest that you make a folder or create a little box full of positive things others have said about you or that you feel about yourself and give it a wonderful "power" name. I called mine "Who knew?" One of the letters in my box is from my first employer after university who wrote me a reference letter. I found it quite by accident when I was clearing out many things I had kept over the years while I was preparing to downsize to a carriage home. I remembered thinking then, and now, how often we cannot know what someone else is thinking; often it is very complimentary. Start today with "the good stuff" and let go of the memories that no longer serve your happiness and your ability to love yourself. We seem to have pessimism covered already with our own negative thoughts—we don't need to add to it by holding onto negative memories.

We can only forgive our past perceived mistakes when we embrace the fact that our choices made sense at the time; we made them with what was available in our minds in the moment. I used to ask each group, "Really, who would make a bad choice on purpose?" I have learned that forgiveness is a healing emotion deep within our soul and judgment is an arrogant one exercised by the ego.

I would like to share this beautiful passage about forgiveness by a Catholic priest, Henri Nouwen:

> Forgiveness is the name of love practiced among people who love poorly. The hard truth is that all of us love poorly. We need to forgive and be forgiven every day, every hour - unceasingly. That is the great work of love among the fellowship of the weak that is the human family. [52]

52 Henri Nouwen, quoted in Oriah Mountain Dreamer, *The Dance* (New York: Thorsons, 2001), 44.

Each of us is part of that family. Self-love requires us to forgive ourselves "unceasingly."

It is not because we grow older and wiser that we gain a new understanding of ourselves. Peace within and renewed hope to create a better tomorrow comes with humility and acceptance. You are simply "human." You are normal. As long as you are still breathing, you have options. We can choose to move beyond our hurt feelings and disappointments in ourselves and begin anew. It has to start within, and we have to let go of any attachment to the timing of the outcomes and our preferred endings. We are blessed with a new day every day; it is the miracle of life and the gift of starting over and the chance to get it right in a different way. We are in a continuous cycle of transforming, becoming empowered, and experiencing renewal.

Although our memory may present more challenges in our quest to give ourselves the same unconditional love golden retrievers express freely, it can also help us discover that trauma in our life can lead to blessings. When I was newly divorced, my feelings of loss and failure were soul destroying for a mother so entrenched in a philosophy of "happily ever after, till death do us part." When I was diagnosed with cancer and told only one in four survived, I struggled with the label that I would forever be a cancer survivor and I would need to move past my fear of uncertainty. At last I understood that everyone's life is uncertain. I was now one of the lucky ones that cherished each day in a new way. Others lived in a fairy tale expecting a "happily ever after" life. I already knew we would all face multiple moments of being blindsided in this nonlinear life of the twenty-first century. Transformation is never optional. However, empowerment is possible with baby steps. Renewal will come in its time—and surprise us.

One day as I processed this life of mine that I could not have imagined, I wrote myself a "letter of compassion"; you may want to do this too. I was thinking that it is so easy to forget and/or minimize the pain that drove us to any actions, and so I began writing:

I accept that I have needs and feelings and they won't always be met. Sometimes these will override my capacity to love myself and to love others. Help me to exercise my ability to choose to forgive and to be forgiven every day—every hour—unceasingly. It is so hard. I slip back so very easily—even when I believe I have tried my best. Sometimes I have no more to give to myself and to others; I disappoint myself. In my frailer moments, all these years later, I still wish I could have stayed and made my marriage work. I remind myself that while compassion makes forgiveness possible, I am still able to choose healthy boundaries, and it doesn't have to be perfect to be perfect. Sometimes that will mean a new beginning.

Unconditional love golden retriever style has an important place in this world. It makes forgiveness possible and I believe it is best served as it relates to self-love. We all seem to need a lot of help when it comes to judging ourselves and thinking we should be perfect. Forgiveness brings healing, judging can keep hate alive, and even a golden retriever sets boundaries; just watch them if another dog tries to steal their ball.

The other day as I sat with my son's golden retriever, I wondered for a moment what he must be thinking. Then I realized he was simply "feeling" our love for each other and I was grateful for the simplicity of the "love lesson." Self-love is the jewel of everything: to be at peace, to love your life, and to feel success on your terms. I encourage you to collaborate with your soul and consider the beauty of the quote by Pablo Casals at the beginning of this chapter: You are indeed "a marvel—you are unique."

It is quotes that have planted the seeds in the garden of my soul all through the years to bring me to my last chapter—"The Magic in Becoming". I hope you are ready to join me.

Insights to Own Who You Are Becoming – Nurturing the Jewel of Self-Love

There is no greater skill you can hone for a peaceful, fulfilled life than to master the ability to love yourself unconditionally. This is a lifetime project! It will surprise you how the ego can intervene and confuse you just when you thought you had overpowered those negative thoughts that enable you to self-sabotage your achievements. Do not be discouraged. They are too deep. Focus on ways to create self-love; it could be as simple as a daily walk or run or bike ride in nature.

In this chapter, I have shared two letters: one is a letter of encouragement and the other of compassion. Write your own letters to yourself and read them often. What steps can you take today to grow your compassion? Is there an important relationship you need to heal? Is it with yourself or someone else? Remember it does not have to be perfect to be perfect. Starting over and moving forward can sometimes mean letting go of what was to find what could be. Could this be like when the first beautiful crocus appears and all the beauty of spring is ahead with no memory of the dark winter we have left behind us? What does a beautiful spring ahead in your life look like for you?

The power of love for me lies in aspiring to love myself and others unconditionally. However, I will always need to make amends when I make mistakes or hurt others and I can still expect the same in return. The words, "I am sorry" are one of the best ways to restart and we can look to the golden retriever who makes loving look so spontaneous and incredibly easy. We do have a choice in determining what we perceive and the feelings we experience. Healing over time may make it possible to change our perceptions. We are still able to choose healthy boundaries that work for us.

Loving ourselves may require that we set boundaries in order to move forward; it is a lifelong work in progress. Think about ways that you have grown and how you have been able to "accept the things you cannot change" and how you are trying to "change the things you can." Read the letters you have written to yourself and fill your heart with the power of forgiveness and compassion. Unconditional love is the hope for our world. It begins with you and me.

Notes to Own Who You Are Becoming:

Chapter 15

The Magic in Becoming

*DREAM…and as you dream remember that only you
can make your dreams come true.
REACH… BELIEVE…There's a wonderful dream waiting just for you.
I know you can make it come true.*

—Larry S Chengges, Springbrook Publications Inc. St Clair Shores, MI

THE MAGIC BEGINS WHEN WE decide to take responsibility and make life about what we can do in this moment to awaken our inner power to be all we can be. Once we embrace the fact that we have choices and begin to feel the power to rise above our doubts and fears, we have a chance to rewrite the ending. We become the architect of our own soul, one baby step at a time.

Transformation is the process of getting through a crisis. It requires significant growth as we navigate huge changes in our lives. Empowerment comes slowly as we heal from the inside out and rediscover what is possible with the tools of gratitude, hope, humility, courage, trust, and self-love. Sometimes the changes are so subtle we might even miss how much we have grown. As we move forward and grow stronger, renewal reveals more ways to awaken our inner power. This is a cycle that may be repeated throughout our lives many times and makes it possible to own who we are becoming.

There are many ways to discover the magic in becoming. In my evolving love story, I have shown you how we can discover insights when we go as far back to the beginning as our memory allows us. It is not about remembering every detail. The meaning of our life can often be found in our stories, not the bare bones of how they have happened, but how we have allowed each story to shape all of our future stories. This can be summed up in one word: perspective. Perspective can change the landscape and create insight from defeat to triumph. The writing of Bernie Glassman demonstrates that those moments when we are broken don't just help lead us to a breakthrough—these can be beautiful opportunities for rebirth and are part of the magic in becoming.

Bernie Glassman's courageous journey to change his perspective and how he found the magic in starting over are a testimony to what can happen with patience and a lot of soul searching and courage. You may want to read "There Are No Words" by Bernie Glassman, in which he discusses his daily practice of bereavement following the sudden death of his wife and dharma partner, Sensei Sandra Jishu Holmes. He shares that when his wife died, "Bernie died, too."[53]. He finds comfort in some of Holmes's written meditations reflecting on when she "had reached a crossroad where 'the old ways of being don't work anymore," as he now found himself "in a state of not-knowing" like she was.[54]

This is often at the core of the challenges for one in transition. We feel as if we have lost our identity and don't know how to become someone new, or even if we can. It can be extremely frightening and at the same time offer an exciting new chapter of hope and renewal. It can finally lead the way to the magic of becoming.

Like Glassman, most people have at least one profoundly earth-shattering event in their lives testing their faith in a better tomorrow. When the world as you knew it now no longer makes sense and you are called upon to draw on every ounce of courage you can, the well-known phrase "the gift of adversity" feels absurd. Furthermore, others may not even understand how difficult it feels to you.

---

53 Bernie Glassman, "There Are No Words," Lion's Roar, January 1, 1998, https://www.lionsroar.com/there-are-no-words/.

54 Glassman, "There Are No Words."

However, to experience the real magic in continuously becoming, one must have felt the earthquake in their soul and feared that suddenly there were now too many pieces to ever put it back together again. You may try to imagine a new start, but it feels impossible. You plan to sleep on it and try again tomorrow. Nope! Tomorrow is not a new day for you. The shattered heart is not responding; it has closed down. It may not have completely given up on all life, but the broken spirit has no tools to restart. It cannot imagine ever feeling joy again. It has decided that life will never be the same again, and indeed it will not.

This last fact can actually be a turning point. We may have first gone through a process of bargaining with our fate and tried in various ways to hold onto the same reality that has changed forever. It is only through acceptance that our former reality is gone that we have a chance to find the magic in starting over.

Throughout this deep narrative by Bernie Glassman, I found there were so many of the concepts I have believed all through my own personal journey from transformation to renewal. Dramatic change demands that we learn how to recognize when we are at a crossroad and realize that part of this will include "not knowing" so many things that once felt so familiar. Old ways don't work anymore, and we may even lose a sense of self and the ability to believe in our future. Without hope to temper the fear of the unknown, we are lost.

Transformation at any time in our life requires that we be still and listen to our innermost thoughts and our instincts. As we humble ourselves and seek help from others, we need to let go of trying to control the outcomes of our actions. The magic in becoming can only be found by taking baby steps every day, no matter how unknown the destination feels. First, we dream of a better tomorrow; then, we reach for ways to realize a new self; finally, we believe in possibilities and move forward with no attachment to the timing.

I remember wondering if I would ever feel happy again. The path of healing leads somewhere in the future that in the present moment of our deepest anguish feels unimaginable. But the "earthquake in our soul" actually becomes the gift to a new life. If the pain is not significant enough, we may just allow life to be stagnant and never find our magic. We may settle for mediocre and let go of our dreams. I once compared the concept of how a tragedy can lead to healing to the faith of a skilled doctor; they can visualize the healing, even as they cut open a person and create a deep wound as a first step. This is a powerful image because our recovery is a process and the pain has to precede the healing and it comes with no guarantees or timelines. As we develop a greater trust in the unknown, we are able to plant the seeds that grow the magic; it seems as if we become what we now believe.

One significant lesson I have learned is that I can contribute to my personal "magic in becoming." I do this by letting go of needing to know how I will find clarity regarding my unanswered questions. The following story reminds us how much is stored in our reservoir of emotions just waiting to be harvested and bring new understanding.

If you are a music lover, you know how a song can transport you back to an exact moment in time and stir all the feelings in your heart again as if it was only yesterday. Throughout the pandemic, I listened to a lot of the popular singers I had loved over the years to find peace in the many hours I spent alone. One song, "Seasons of the Heart," started to play, and the beautiful lyrics came up on my phone as I listened to John Denver's wonderful rendition. Suddenly tears began to flow down my cheeks and all of a sudden, I was sobbing. It wasn't from grief. I realized it was from a place of gratitude. Over twenty years after my divorce, this amazing song spoke to my soul and gave me my answer: "No there was no way I could have saved my marriage."

When I heard this song and read the beautiful words, I felt at peace and knew I was right to leave my marriage, and I finally understood how much I had healed. The magic in becoming can often sneak up on us. Suddenly, perhaps with a song, we are struck with a wonderful, unexpected moment when we realize how far we have transformed and grown. There it is, an answer to a difficult question we have held in our hearts for so long. I believe there are many ways we can strengthen the connection to the longings deep within our soul. Once we discover what works best for us, it will open the door to greater possibilities for peace, joy, and love to fill our lives.

Seeking out music that I loved was certainly effective for me in this moment. Meditation is another helpful practice, especially in nature or relaxing with your favorite pet. Discover the magnets to reach your inner voice. Promise yourself you will stay open to every small sign. Embrace them as I did when the lyrics of "Seasons of the Heart" reached my soul.

Sometimes another person's perception of who we are can lead us to a magical moment where we realize how far we have come. There are two important truths in communication: "nothing is ever what it seems" and "what I think they are thinking may not be at all what they are thinking." Here is a dramatic story to illustrate this. It was the most upsetting and explosive opening session with a brand-new group I had ever experienced in my time as a career coach. I had started the training with the same message for at least six months. My own personal circumstances were still very challenging, making me emotionally fragile, even as I tried to always put on a brave and professional face.

Suddenly, a man burst forth in front of the whole group, yelling at me, "What would you know about struggle and pain and job loss? You with your perfect job and your perfect life. How dare you talk about taking us on an adventure to a new life? Who are you to even think you know what we are all going through, and how can you even begin to relate to our losses, defeats, loneliness, and failures?" Ironically, although he could not know, I was also experiencing these things too. Of course he could not know, because "nothing is ever what it seems."

We never learned anything more about this man's struggles because he left before lunch. Although this event was difficult, it was also invaluable, and the whole group bonded in a special way, even though we could not know what each other was thinking. It gave me the opportunity to share that we are not here to judge each other and perhaps make false assumptions. What we can know for sure is that everyone carries a burden deep within their heart and that we will all benefit with the unconditional support from each other. Part of the magic in becoming occurs during watershed moments that happen as we grow and heal.

In the middle of this dramatic verbal attack directed at me I actually felt at peace with how much I had healed. This whole experience reminded me that as we evolve into who we are capable of becoming, others may never know how difficult our journey has been. Often only we are aware of the wonder of our life to this point. I now no longer saw myself as one of my clients; I had reached a new level of acceptance and owned who I had become.

Sometimes there can be magic in becoming very early on in the midst of your challenges to transform and heal. Clarity can come when we least expect it. This happened one day for me when I was walking from the parking lot to work and my mind was filled with the ongoing struggles of being in the middle of my divorce. Suddenly, a milestone moment dominated my thoughts: "Maybe there is no 'happily ever after' for anyone; maybe life is about living 'happily every day.' What if this is my finest hour so far?"

I wondered where this revelation came from and how I had reached this new perspective? The passage of time and an ever-active subconscious mind can collaborate to influence our thoughts. To be able to describe what you initially felt was your "biggest personal failure" as "your finest hour," before the ink on the divorce papers was even dry, is magic. It makes it possible for you to validate the reasons and the courage it took to get this far and own it all.

So what are some of the ways we can create a "happily every day" life in the midst of a divorce or any other life crisis? Please bear with me while I share how I was able to embrace the magic of becoming and rationalize a wonderful, extravagant purchase in the middle of one of the greatest crises I had ever faced. I had found a delightful, whimsical gift store near my work, and I often walked there on my lunch hour to fill my heart and mind with fun moments amidst an intense day. There I spotted the most amazing Winnie the Pooh bookends. There was absolutely no reason I had to buy them, but I LOVED them. I told myself that not only were they too expensive, but they would also take up two-thirds of a book shelf, which was intended for books, not ornaments or bookends!

One day, I discovered that they were on sale. I delivered very distracted workshops that afternoon, and yes, you guessed it, I went back after work and bought them. To this day, they still fill my heart with joy and they still take up significant space on the bookshelf—however I am not advocating you go out and spend money you don't have just to please your soul. And yet there are times when, if we do take action on a whim, it may become a turning point in our ability to move beyond the pain. Suddenly we find ourselves feeling joy again. It is important to remember that as we grow through transformation to renewal, honoring what brings us happiness is a magical part of the journey.

Everything we have discussed thus far, as well as all the previous fourteen insights, all hold some of the magic in becoming. "Transformation is never optional" is a phrase that best describes every person's life journey. It happens with patience and courage when we are able to complete an important passage from not knowing to discovering our truth. We do not empower ourselves and own who we are becoming by abandoning our past or hiding from it. Instead, we decide the past no longer defines us, and finally we reach a level of gratitude and come to understand that without it all, we would not be the incredible person we are. We are able to create a sanctuary of peace inside that slowly gives us the ability to accept, forgive, start over, and actually value everything, the good, the bad, and the ugly.

Think of the verb "transform" as "the act of changing one's beliefs." Healing and finding out who we really could become can be as simple as changing how we tell the story about ourselves to our soul. One day, a burst of power causes us to say, "I am not who you think I am, I am not who I thought I was, I am not who I want to be, and I am not who I could become!" One day, the only thought that consumes us is that life is short and only happens once; we feel driven to find ways to get it right.

I invite you to embrace the power of storytelling, a captivating way to teach and learn. Explore the deeper messages that the details of my stories may sometimes overshadow. Look for the hidden nuggets of a story that resonate with you. Gently let your story unravel and intertwine with mine to take you on a healing journey from transformation through empowerment to renewal. Experience the magic as you come to trust there will be a tsunami of people, places, books, events, and other unknowns that work together to make the once seemingly impossible now possible. This can happen many times.

My hope is that my stories can encourage you, the reader, to take responsibility for all the ways you have told and retold your story to yourself. I have found that the magic in becoming lies in our storytelling abilities and how they fuel our power to rise above our circumstances, rewrite our endings, and reach for our future dreams. We may need the help of family, friends and even professional guidance to show us how our story can serve us in the best possible way and, most importantly, reflect the truth with a non-judgment perspective.

At the center of every story, there is a hero or a villain that defines the theme. Think about how you have described yourself in your story and if you have laid out the facts correctly. The yin and yang of the gift of our mind is the power it has to deny what is true and to believe what is not valid. Explore where you may have made your story fiction and gently try to help yourself to climb back up the mountain to non-fiction so you are working with reality.

Even with professional counselling to help us uncover our truth, we need to embrace it or it won't help us to heal. What matters next is how we apply our truth and use it to reach for what is possible in our quest to find the magic in becoming. If you recall the lady who carried around her poor employee evaluation years later, you might see that she was being the villain in her own story. Her truth was skewed by her poor self-esteem, and it was difficult for her to hear anyone else's thoughts that might help her to let go of how she wrote her own story.

There was another big part of the story of this employee's evaluation that she was not including in her story; this was the only poor evaluation in her entire career. The multiple baby steps we will need to take as we grow into our own empowered self will require that we simultaneously develop a deep love of self. This is an example of how empowerment and renewal are not exclusive stand-alone parts of the magic. They intertwine and overlap, and sometimes we fall back on some of the components of transformation.

Some of my titles in each section of my book became my "mantras" and questions to draw me back into believing in life. Even as I am writing this book, I am reminded to "Learn to listen to my soul" and trust that "Courage finds a way." When the ever-so-strong ego on my shoulder causes me to doubt myself and it feels as if I may crumble, I ask, "What if it is possible to heal?" and "What could happen if I try?"

You might think that my purchase of the Winnie the Pooh book ends was just a whimsical story. In fact, it was far more significant. I responded to my soul's desire for irrational joy. Looking back, I think it was a turning point for me to realize that now I could have the final say to my happiness, however frivolous another might judge it to be. To find the magic in starting over, we need to honor the fact that we have earned this moment, paid our dues, and already proven that we can successfully move forward because we already have, however small the baby steps might have been to get here.

Once we start to experience small moments of magic in starting over, courage will begin to replace some of the fear. The exciting moment is when we begin to trust that the most amazing possibilities are too great for us to even predict. Life dares us to own who we are becoming and celebrate every step. It was the angels disguised as strangers and the often bizarre moments of synchronicity along the way that often kept my feet to the fire and reminded me to trust that if they happened even once, they could happen again.

I have written a book to share my personal journey in discovering my magic in becoming. Now it is your turn to begin the archeological dig to start over and excavate your potential. It begins with new choices and how you decide to craft your story. Although so much of the work to uncover the magic in becoming and to own who you are becoming can only be done by you, you cannot do it alone. It is a process that begins both deep within you and all around you. My journey began with the help of a professional therapist and would not have been possible without the support of my family, friends, children, and a Power greater than myself. When you show up, pay attention, trust the process, and let go of the delivery details, you cannot help but experience your own magic; gradually, you will uncover your own insights to become "braver than you believe."[55]

Your greatest glory (and mine) is when we become empowered from within and the details don't matter anymore, even though they are still somewhere inside our soul. There might have been fear and trauma, but now we can feel the sunlight inside beckoning us to try. We are finally filled with a deep compassion for ourselves, our place in life, and for everyone

---

55 *Pooh's Grand Adventure: The Search for Christopher Robin*, directed by Carter Crocker and Karl Geurs (1997; Glendale, CA: Walt Disney Television Animation)

in it. The possibilities in life grow as we become more and more able to approach any new significant setback and still feel a semblance of control. This is how we create a better future for ourselves and for those around us.

There will always be a deep hole somewhere in the sidewalk of life, as we read in the poem[56] in chapter seven. As you strive to become empowered and renewed, you may gradually find yourself in a place of continuous optimism where you can know, even without knowing, that this too will pass. You will learn to embrace that you are the hero in your own story. Your tools will be gratitude, hope, humility, trust, courage and always, the jewel of self-love.

Think about your evolving love story and what owning who you are becoming means to you. One time a client wrote on a thank-you card to me: "Now that I own myself, I am emotionally debt-free." In this message, I found it so profound how she chose to describe what "owning who she was becoming" meant to her. Only you have learned over the years the price you have paid for betraying your authentic self. It is not a selfish act when we put ourselves first; it is similar to the instructions on the airplane to parents: "Put your oxygen mask on first."

Make life about what you can do in this moment to awaken your inner power to be all you can be. Know you can do it, whatever "it" might be. This is key in growing your ability to move forward. You have the power to rise above your doubts and fears, your disappointments and perceived failures. Exercise your choices. You can rewrite your ending every day and you can become the architect of your soul, one baby step at a time, until you achieve the jewel of self-love, unconditional love golden retriever style.

Own who you are becoming. Dare to reconcile your soul with all the things and people and places in your past. Open yourself to miracles and love; it all has to start with you.

---

56 Nelson, "Autobiography in Five Short Chapters," *There's a Hole in My Sidewalk*, xi-xii.

Insights to Own Who You Are Becoming – Creating Your Own Magic

Find a way to be excited about something. We used to talk about the word "enthus-iasm" in the career program and how it meant "I am sold myself." For many, the word "excited" is not part of their comfortable vocabulary; it is too strong. OK then; use another word that means you can feel the value. It could be about your pet, your favorite dessert, your special hiking or running trail, gardening, and so on. Once we can identify anything at all that matters to us, we can begin the journey on the road to own who we are becoming.

I saw this so many times in the people I coached who had lost what sometimes seemed like everything that had the potential to bring them any kind of joy or personal satisfaction. I remember the lady who was so grateful to have been accepted into the program at her age. She wrote in her thank-you card that she didn't realize that she would be celebrating her eighty-sixth birthday with so many great people, who even bought her a cake! We were all in awe of her parting message: "Trying to find a job at my age is a challenge, but I will keep at it." Now that is one extraordinary human being from whom we can all learn! Her enthusiasm for life and possibilities was incredible. She had the magic sauce—hope!

Start a road map of your life stories thus far using the section titles of this book: Transformation is Never Optional, Empowerment in Baby Steps, and Renewal Will Surprise You. To break this project down into small "bites" for your outline, list the headings of the insights at the end of each chapter so they can trigger your mind with personal stories. Here they are:

✓ Building on Self Knowledge
✓ Recovering is not the Same as Curing
✓ Connecting with Your Inner Voice
✓ Shifting to the Power of Hope
✓ Believing in a New Dream
✓ Remembering Your Strengths
✓ Committing to Showing Up
✓ Trusting in Happy Endings

✓ Feeling Your Power in the Fear
✓ Knowing How Much is Unknown
✓ Expecting to be Surprised
✓ Learning from Mother Nature
✓ Finding Special Nuggets in Everyone
✓ Nurturing the Jewel of Self-Love
✓ Creating Your Own Magic

This may seem like a "book" project. However, this road map is actually a way each of us can better understand our journey. This could enable us to create our own magic when we process how fragile today is and how much it is affected by our internal thoughts.

Are you open to replacing "happily ever after" with "happily every day"? To believe we can transform ourselves, become empowered and experience renewal over and over again is the ultimate journey to finding peace. We can know by our own life stories that we have what we need to become all that we are meant to be.

Discover what you have been given and share it with the world! Can you imagine how Michael J. Fox, already an accomplished young actor with a whole lifetime of success ahead of him, felt when he was diagnosed with Parkinson's disease at twenty-nine? Now at the age of sixty-plus, when he reunited with his colleague Christopher Lloyd from *Back to the Future*, this is the message of courage that he shared for us all to emulate:

> Parkinson's is the gift that keeps on taking—but it's a gift, and I wouldn't change it for anything . . . People like Chris have been there a lot for me, and so many of you have. It's not about what I have, it's about what I have been given, the voice to get this done, and help people out.[57]

---

57 Michael J. Fox, "Michael J. Fox Says 'Back to the Future III' Sparked Christopher Lloyd Friendship: 'A Great Guy,'" by Glenn Garner, *People*, January 22, 2023, https://people.com/movies/
michael-j-fox-back-to-the-future-iii-sparked-christopher-lloyd-friendship/.

Very few people are called upon to rise above such challenges, but the message can inspire us all. I believe that the heroic story we know of Michael J. Fox came about because he has mastered the tools I have referenced before in this book: gratitude, hope, humility, courage, and trust. We know that "nothing is what it seems," and that life for each of us will always be a nonlinear journey, just as it has been for Michael J. Fox. We can draw on his inspiring example to create our own magic on the road to own who we are becoming.

Everyone writing from memories, in a journal or for a memoir, will uncover a greater clarity once they have had time to heal to a level of objectivity. In looking back, we are now ready to move forward. This is the moment we can ask, "What did I learn?" "How did I grow?" "Who did I become that made me more than I ever could have imagined?" "How have I used my loss, grief, betrayal, persecution, and the multitude of changes in my life?" Gradually, we will uncover the magic in our stories that enabled us to become the unique person we are now, and who we could still become.

How can you augment your solo work on healing with the many support networks available? Beyond the benefits of professional help, there are many other organizations that make it possible for like-minded people to help each other rebuild their lives and make the journey easier. In addition, there is healing in sharing our story with others and helping those whose challenges sometimes mirror ours.

In the end, which is now the beginning, it is up to each of us to discover our magic in becoming. My next chapter will depend on how I have chosen to frame the pictures of my life and the stories I have written to enhance the photographs in my mind, heart, and soul. The gifts I have found each time that I needed to start over have inspired me to share them with you. Trust in the unknown grew with each unexpected challenge, and in our nonlinear world, it is a given we will all need to start over often. Perhaps the abundance of gifts allotted to me, an ordinary person, will encourage you to take a second look, dig deeper, and much to your surprise, you too will discover gifts once hidden that now give meaning and purpose to so many of your milestone memories.

Thank you for reading my stories and the insights that grew when I put them into a book. I look forward to learning about the person you are becoming, the gifts you have found, and the success you have achieved every time you started over in this unpredictable and yet amazingly wonderful world of ours.

Embrace the magic in life's ongoing journey of transformation, empowerment, and renewal.

Notes to Own Who You Are Becoming:

Notes to Own Who You Are Becoming:

Notes to Own Who You Are Becoming:

Printed in Canada